"十四五"高等教育英语精品课程系列教材

华南理工大学出版基金资助项目

中国文化阅读教程

主　编　战双鹃　徐阳子　谢宝霞
副主编　方久华　车思琪　屈　薇　张琳琳　许文丽

·广州·

图书在版编目（CIP）数据

中国文化阅读教程：英文、汉文 / 战双鹃，徐阳子，谢宝霞主编 . —广州：华南理工大学出版社，2023.12

ISBN 978-7-5623-7509-8

Ⅰ . ①中… Ⅱ . ①战… ②徐… ③谢… Ⅲ . 中华文化–教材–英、汉 Ⅳ . ①K203

中国国家版本馆CIP数据核字（2023）第243874号

中国文化阅读教程

战双鹃　徐阳子　谢宝霞　主编

出 版 人：柯　宁
出版发行：华南理工大学出版社
　　　　　（广州五山华南理工大学17号楼，邮编510640）
　　　　　http://hg.cb.scut.edu.cn　E-mail: scutc13@scut.edu.cn
　　　　　营销部电话：020-87113487　87111048（传真）
责任编辑：陈　蓉
责任校对：马远远
印 刷 者：佛山家联印刷有限公司
开　　本：787mm×1092mm　1/16　印张：8　字数：201千
版　　次：2023年12月第1版　印次：2023年12月第1次印刷
定　　价：39.00元

版权所有　盗版必究　　印装差错　负责调换

前　言

《大学英语教学指南（2020版）》明确指出，"大学英语课程可培养学生对中国文化的理解和阐释能力，服务中国文化对外传播；社会主义核心价值观应有机融入大学英语教学内容；课程需在课程建设、教材编写、教学实施等各个环节充分挖掘其思想和情感资源，丰富其人文内涵，实现工具性和人文性的有机统一"。本教材的编写体现新时代要求，符合外语教学服务国家社会与人才培养的根本宗旨，可发挥外语教材在高等院校外语教学落实立德树人根本任务中的载体作用。

相较于传统的英语阅读教材，本教材在立意与内容等方面进行了更新与优化。教材选取的内容凸显中华优秀传统文化与社会主义核心价值观，彰显我国新时代发展风貌，帮助学生了解中国的新发展、新面貌，引领学生深刻理解中国文化深邃的价值与中国发展对世界的深远影响，着力通过篇章内容的价值引领坚定学生的中国立场，增强学生的文化自信。

本教材以篇章阅读的方式呈现中国发展新面貌，选材涵盖中国文化知识主题板块，包括以下八个单元：第一单元介绍中国智慧；第二单元介绍中国式现代化；第三单元介绍中国科学技术；第四单元介绍中国经济；第五单元介绍中国环境；第六单元介绍中国建筑；第七单元介绍中国工艺美术；第八单元介绍中国传统节日。每个单元由两篇阅读文章及一篇拓展阅读组成，文章主要选自中国国际电视台、国务院新闻办公室官网、中国日报网等主流媒体的最新英语语料，涵盖代表中国新发展的主要内容和当前的热点话题。每篇文章包含不同类型的练习题，包括单词练习、篇章理解、段落翻译、主题讨论等，涵盖语言知识、中国元素主题、中国文化价值与内涵等，旨在提升学生的英语理解与应用能力，尤其是对中国文化与中国当今风貌的理解以及用英语传播中国文化的能力，并帮助学生树立正确的世界观、人生观和价值观，提高学生传播中国文化价值观的素养与能力。

本教材设计突出启发性和思辨性，在结构编排上从易到难，强调内容多样性与评价多维度，从选材到练习设计均有机融入课程思政元素，以系统培养学生的国际视野、家国情怀与使命担当。教材强调英语语言学习与文化价值学习、文化对外传播交流相结合，力求突出英语语言学习的人文性、社会性与实用性，彰显外语教育的价值内核，强调学生参与和深度学习的实践。

　　本教材主要供普通高等院校本科生大学英语公共基础课、中国文化类通识课、中西文化对比等课程的课堂教学与课外阅读学习使用，也适合研究生及广大英语学习爱好者阅读使用。本教材凝聚了全体编写人员的努力和付出。在教材编写过程中，华南理工大学外国语学院研究生汤晓钰、李芷晴、李皓玥参与了部分文献资料的整理工作，在此深表感谢。由于水平所限，编写内容难免存在疏漏，敬请使用本教材的老师和同学们对存在的不足提出意见和建议。

编　者

2023年8月

CONTENTS

Unit 1　Chinese Wisdom ··· 1

 Text A　How China Aims to Benefit World with "Shared Future" Vision ········ 1
 Text B　What China's Green Transition Means for the World ······················ 6
 Further Reading　China: from Follower to Leader in the Digital Economy · 12

Unit 2　Chinese Modernization ··· 15

 Text A　China Forges Ahead on Chinese Path to Modernization ···················· 15
 Text B　China's Modernization Promotes Global Peace and Development ···· 21
 Further Reading　Nation's Modernization Drive Attracts Global Attention ·· 26

Unit 3　China's Science and Technology ··· 31

 Text A　What Does China's Innovation-Driven Development Strategy Mean
     for the World? ··· 31
 Text B　China Pursues Self-Reliant Sci-Tech Progress to Benefit All ············ 37
 Further Reading　Cooperation Key to Speed up Tech Breakthroughs ·········· 44

Unit 4　China's Economy ·· 46

 Text A　A Look at China's Economic Resilience amid Sluggish Global
     Growth ·· 46
 Text B　China Ramps up Macro Control for Stable Economic Growth ·········· 52
 Further Reading　Globalization of Renminbi to Boost Stability ···················· 58

Unit 5　China's Environment ··· 60

 Text A　Guideline Targets Health of Yangtze ·· 60
 Text B　Green Lifestyle Gains Traction Among China's Gen Z ····················· 67

Further Reading   Eco Forum Global Highlights China's Contribution to Harmony Between Man, Nature ········· 73

Unit 6   China's Architecture ········· 75

Text A   Traditional Chinese Earthen Buildings Inspire Modern Society ········ 75
Text B   Reviving Ancient Architecture ········· 81
Further Reading   Tibetan Relics Show Solid Bonds Between Plateau and Plains ········· 88

Unit 7   China's Arts and Crafts ········· 90

Text A   Chinese Embroidery ········· 90
Text B   Calligraphy, the Gem of Chinese Culture ········· 96
Further Reading   China Focus: Shipwreck Archaeology Unveils Glory of Maritime Silk Road ········· 101

Unit 8   China's Customs and Festivals ········· 103

Text A   Chinese Festival Going Global with Dragon Boats ········· 103
Text B   Customs Around the Mid-Autumn Festival ········· 109
Further Reading   The Qixi Festival Is More than Chinese Valentine's Day ········· 114

Keys to Exercises ········· 116

Unit 1

Chinese Wisdom

Text A

How China Aims to Benefit World with "Shared Future" Vision

The week-long 20th National Congress of the Communist Party of China has concluded, with a blueprint mapped out for China's future development in the next five years and beyond. CGTN is publishing "How China Works — Charting the Future," a special series delving deep into a key report adopted at the congress, to see how the country can fulfill the goals and tasks on the new journey of the new era.

China is committed to building a human community with a shared future because it believes that it is the best path forward for all the world's people.

As an ancient Chinese philosopher observed, "all living things may grow side by side without harming one another, and different roads may run in parallel without interfering with one another."

In a report to the 20th National Congress of the Communist Party of China (CPC), Xi Jinping, general secretary of the CPC Central Committee, stressed that while China has always been committed to the foreign policy goals of upholding world peace and promoting common development, it is now also dedicated to creating a human community with a shared future.

Only when all countries pursue the cause of common good, live in harmony and engage in cooperation for mutual benefit will there be sustained prosperity and guaranteed security, the report said.

A "Shared Future" for All

President Xi first brought the notion of "a community with a shared future for mankind" to the world's attention during a 2013 speech at the Moscow State Institute of International Relations.

"Mankind, by living in the same global village within the same time and space where history and reality meet, have increasingly emerged as a community of common destiny in which everyone has in himself a little bit of others," he said.

In recent years, the world has been challenged by a rise in global crises that bind the fate of nations together closer than ever, from climate change to the COVID-19 pandemic. To effectively address them, governments must come together and take collective and coherent action.

In 2022, the devastating consequences of climate change were evident for all to see as frequent extreme weather events battered every corner of the globe. Unprecedented heatwaves swept Europe, causing destructive wildfires, severe droughts and thousands of deaths. In Pakistan, severe flooding put one-third of the country under water and damaged 1.8 million homes. In the U.S., powerful hurricanes left thousands of families homeless.

"Acknowledging a shared future demands that all of us challenge poor environmental decisions made by businesses or governments," wrote Anthony Moretti, associate professor at Robert Morris University in the U.S. state of Pennsylvania, in an opinion piece for CGTN.

One of the major goals of building a human community with a shared future is for nations to achieve win-win cooperation, a concept best demonstrated by the China-initiated Belt and Road Initiative (BRI).

Since its introduction in 2013, the BRI has substantially boosted trade and investment activities throughout the world. The annual trade volume between China and the nearly 150 BRI participating countries expanded from $1.04 trillion in 2013 to $1.8 trillion in 2021 — a leap of 73 percent over eight years.

Under the initiative, China has brought its broad experience in manufacturing, telecommunication, infrastructure development and other areas to less-developed regions and countries, helping create numerous new jobs in local economies.

According to a World Bank report, the initiative has the potential to lift 7.6 million people out of extreme poverty and 32 million out of moderate poverty globally while boosting trade by 2.8 to 9.7 percent for participating countries and by 1.7 to 6.2 percent for the whole world.

Besides the BRI, China is also inviting countries around the world to take part in implementing two other initiatives in order to realize a "shared future," namely the Global Development Initiative and Global Security Initiative.

"We will work with peoples of all other countries to champion humanity's shared values of peace, development, fairness, justice, democracy and freedom to safeguard global peace and promote global development, and keep promoting the building of a human community with a shared future," Xi said when meeting the press at the Great Hall of the People in Beijing in October.

(Source: https://news.cgtn.com/news/2022-11-13/How-China-aims-to-benefit-world-with-shared-future-vision-1eVa39UCWpq/index.html)

Language Focus

Words and Expressions

delve v. 钻研，探究	to carry on intensive and thorough research for data, information, or the like
interfere v. 干扰，阻碍	come between so as to be hindrance or obstacle
uphold v. 支持，维护	keep or maintain in unaltered condition
dedicate v. 致力，献身	give entirely to a specific person, activity, or cause
prosperity n. 繁荣，成功	be at the high point in one's career or reach a high point in historical significance or importance
destiny n. 命运，天意	an event (or a course of events) that will inevitably happen in the future
pandemic n. 大流行病	an epidemic that is geographically widespread; occurring throughout a region or even throughout the world
devastate v. 毁坏，破坏	cause extensive destruction or ruin utterly
batter v. 连续猛击；肆虐	to hit somebody/something hard many times, especially in a way that causes serious damage
unprecedented adj. 前所未有的，史无前例的	without previous instance; never before known or experienced
destructive adj. 破坏性的，毁灭性的	something that is capable of causing great damage, harm, or injury

poverty *n.* 贫穷，贫困		the state of having little or no money and few or no material possessions
moderate *adj.* 普通的；中等的； 适度的，有节制的		being within reasonable or average limits; not excessive or extreme
implement *v.* 执行，贯彻		apply in a manner consistent with its purpose or design

Notes and Explanations

➤ a community with a shared future for mankind 人类命运共同体：习近平主席提出的重要外交理念，新时代中国特色社会主义基本方略的重要内容之一。构建人类命运共同体，基本内涵就是建设持久和平、普遍安全、共同繁荣、开放包容、清洁美丽的世界。

➤ Belt and Road Initiative (BRI) "一带一路"倡议："丝绸之路经济带"和"21世纪海上丝绸之路"的简称。在"一带一路"建设国际合作框架内，各方秉持共商、共建、共享原则，携手应对世界经济面临的挑战，开创发展新机遇，谋求发展新动力，拓展发展新空间，实现优势互补、互利共赢，不断朝着人类命运共同体方向迈进。

➤ Global Development Initiative 全球发展倡议：习近平主席在第七十六届联合国大会上提出的全球性倡议。倡议内容包括：坚持发展优先；坚持以人民为中心；坚持普惠包容；坚持创新驱动；坚持人与自然和谐共生；坚持行动导向。

➤ Global Security Initiative 全球安全倡议：习近平主席在博鳌亚洲论坛2022年年会开幕式上郑重提出的倡议，系统阐述了中方促进世界安危与共、维护世界和平安宁的立场主张，强调人类是不可分割的安全共同体。这一重大倡议明确回答了"世界需要什么样的安全理念、各国怎样实现共同安全"的时代课题，为应对国际安全挑战提供了中国方案。

Exercises

1. Dealing with Unfamiliar Words

Match the words in the left with their definitions.

(1) blueprint   a meeting of elected or appointed representatives

(2) pandemic   a successful, flourishing, or thriving condition

(3) congress   an important act or statement that is intended to solve a problem

(4) harmony   a detailed outline or plan of action

(5) initiative	the basic structure or features of a system or organization
(6) prosperity	systems used in transmitting messages over a distance electronically
(7) infrastructure	an epidemic that is geographically widespread
(8) telecommunication	a consistent, orderly, or pleasing arrangement of parts

2. Reading and Understanding

Decide whether the following statements are true (T) or false (F).

(1) It is believed that a human community with a shared future is the best path forward for all the world's people.

(2) Extreme weather events will have no impact on the global economy.

(3) The BRI is an ambitious effort to improve regional cooperation and connectivity on a trans-continental scale.

(4) How to respond effectively to global crises is a common challenge for governments and international organizations.

(5) Global Development Initiative and Global Security Initiative are proposed at the same time by China.

3. Questions for Discussion

Work in small groups and discuss the following questions.

(1) What will "building a community of a shared future for mankind" bring to the world?

(2) How does the Belt and Road Initiative help developing countries?

(3) How will higher education change in the post-pandemic future?

4. Translating

Translate the following paragraph into English.

当今世界面临着百年未有之大变局，政治多极化、经济全球化、文化多样化和社会信息化潮流不可逆转，各国间的联系和依存日益加深，但也面临诸多共同挑战。粮食安全、资源短缺、气候变化、网络攻击、人口爆炸、环境污染、疾病流行、跨国犯罪等全球非传统安全问题层出不穷，对国际秩序和人类生存都构成了严峻挑战。不论人们身处何国、信仰如何、是否愿意，实际上已经处在一个命运共同体中。与此同时，一种以应对人类共同挑战为目的的全球价值观已开始形成，并逐步获得国际共识。

Text B

What China's Green Transition Means for the World

Lucid waters and lush mountains are invaluable assets.

This philosophy for green and sustainable development has well depicted one of the defining features of China in the new era. It means that Beijing, when pushing forward China's development, is committed to maintaining harmony between humanity and nature.

Under such a guideline, China's green transition is rapidly gaining momentum, from developing non-fossil energy to updating the industrial structure, from investing in low-carbon technologies to transforming the transport sector.

What has China achieved in its green shift? How is it benefiting both China's industries as well as others around the world in terms of environmental protection and development opportunities?

Low Carbon

China has established a carbon neutralization working mechanism to implement the "dual carbon" goal, which is to peak carbon dioxide emissions before 2030 and achieve carbon neutrality before 2060. It has clarified the top-level design of the "dual carbon" work, and formulated implementation plans in energy, industry, transportation as well as other key areas.

Over the past years, China has taken concrete steps to optimize its energy mix, in which renewable energy has played a more significant role.

Data show that the installed capacity of renewable energy has surpassed one billion kilowatts, accounting for 44.8 percent of China's overall installed capacity. The installed capacity of hydropower, wind power, and photovoltaic power each exceeded 300 million kilowatts, all ranking the highest in the world, according to a white paper titled "China's Green Development in the New Era", released by China's State Council Information Office in January.

From 2012 to 2021, China's annual energy consumption growth rate of 3 percent supported an average economic growth rate of 6.6 percent, carbon dioxide emissions per unit of GDP decreased by about 34.4 percent, and energy consumption per unit of GDP decreased by 26.4 percent, with a cumulative saving of 1.4 billion tons of standard coal.

In 2021, China's national carbon market officially launched online trading, covering 4.5 billion tons of greenhouse gas emissions annually, making it the world's largest carbon market. It has encouraged companies to reduce their carbon emissions by putting a price on carbon, and drive the development of low-carbon technologies.

"China's low-carbon strategy was laudable," said Phay Siphan, Cambodian government's chief spokesman. "It truly demonstrates China's commitment to promoting global carbon emissions reduction and green development."

Opportunities for Everyone

Green is the new gold. As China is transitioning towards a greener development mode, low-carbon industries in the country have been flourishing in recent years, which has spawned more business opportunities for enterprises worldwide.

The new energy vehicle (NEV) industry is a fine illustration. Last year alone, China sold about 6.89 million NEVs, skyrocketing 93.4 percent year on year. NEV production soared 96.9 percent from a year earlier to about 7.06 million units. The market share of NEVs in China's auto market reached 25.6 percent in 2022, up 12.1 percentage points from 2021.

Thanks to China's thriving NEV market, Mercedes-Benz increased its deliveries of NEVs by 143 percent year on year in 2022. Hubertus Troska, member of the board of management of Mercedes-Benz Group AG responsible for Greater China, said last month that the German carmaker will continue to invest more in China.

"We will expand our layout of R&D and industry chain and accelerate our innovative transformation towards electrification, digitalization, and carbon neutrality to meet the upgrading luxury mobility needs of Chinese customers," Troska said in an interview with Xinhua.

Citing China's ever-growing portion of the global electric vehicle market, Leslie Maasdorp, vice president and chief financial officer of the New Development Bank, said China can play a crucial role in stimulating the low-carbon growth strategy of the world economy.

A Shared Green Future

Domestically, China's green transition is bringing a real change. Globally, it is also helping other countries to sustain green growth.

In the mostly arid, desert-capped Kenyan county of Garissa, a China-financed solar power plant, the largest solar plant in East and Central Africa, has set Kenya on the path of achieving green energy sufficiency, and brought benefits to thousands of families and businesses since 2019.

"China is the largest supplier of solar energy equipment across the world and in Africa in particular," said Ajay Mathur, director general of the International Solar Alliance.

While noting that many solar panels and batteries being used in Africa are of Chinese origin, Mathur underscored China's involvement and huge potential in terms of realizing Africa's quest for solar energy development.

"There is the greatest linkage that exists between the Chinese manufacturers of solar energy technology and the African users of that technology," he said.

Apart from African countries, China is also sharing its green development philosophy with many more countries across the globe. The Chilean capital of Santiago has been tapping electric vehicles from China as part of plans to revamp its public transport system and advance clean mobility.

While boosting development, maintaining biological diversity is also emphasized. For example, many tunnels were extended and roads replaced by bridges to protect elephant habitats in the construction of the China-Laos Railway.

"The contribution of China's green development to global sustainable development cannot be ignored, and it also sets an example for other countries' green development," said Abdulrahman Aldakhil, director of Corporate Communication of Saudi National Center for Vegetation Cover Development Combating Desertification.

"China's promotion of international cooperation to protect the environment is a manifestation of its sense of responsibility," he said. "China's experience in green development is worth learning from."

(Source: http://english.scio.gov.cn/in-depth/2023-03/14/content_85166669.htm)

Language Focus

Words and Expressions

transition n. 过渡，转变，转型	the act of passing from one state or place to the next
momentum n. 推进力，动力，势头	an impelling force or strength
optimize v. 优化，使更优化，充分利用	make optimal; get the most out of; use best
surpass v. 超过，胜过，优于	be greater in scope or size than some standard
hydropower n. 水力发电	hydroelectric power is derived from the energy of falling water and running water

cumulative *adj.* 积累的，渐增的		increasing by successive addition
laudable *adj.* 值得赞赏的		worthy of high praise
skyrocket *v.* 飞涨，猛涨		shoot up abruptly, like a rocket
arid *adj.* 干燥的，干旱的		lacking sufficient water or rainfall
underscore *v.* 强调，加强		draw attention to the thing and emphasize its importance
quest *v.* 寻求，探求		the act of searching for something
revamp *v.* 修改，翻新，改进		to patch up or renovate; repair or restore
vegetation *n.* （总称）植物，植被		all the plant life in a particular region or period

Notes and Explanations

➢ green transition 绿色转型：指以生态文明建设为主导，以循环经济为基础，以绿色管理为保障，发展模式向可持续发展转变，实现资源节约，环境友好，生态平衡，人、自然、社会和谐发展。

➢ "dual carbon" goals "双碳"目标：指中国提出的2030年前实现"碳达峰"与2060年前实现"碳中和"的目标。"双碳"战略倡导绿色、环保、低碳的生活方式，持续推进产业结构和能源结构调整，大力发展可再生能源，加快降低碳排放步伐，有利于引导绿色技术创新，提高产业和经济的全球竞争力。

➢ energy consumption 能源消费：指生产和生活所消耗的能源，是衡量一个国家经济发展和人民生活水平的重要标志。能源消费强度变化与工业化进程密切相关。随着人口的增长、经济的发展、日益提高的能源消费水平，能源问题日益突出，能源消费的宏观管理和优化利用就显得尤为重要。

➢ green development 绿色发展：是顺应自然、促进人与自然和谐共生的发展，是用最少资源环境代价取得最大经济社会效益的发展，是高质量、可持续的发展，已经成为各国共识。党的十八大以来，我国坚持走生态优先、绿色发展的道路，创造了举世瞩目的生态奇迹和绿色发展奇迹，美丽中国建设迈出重大步伐。

Exercises

1. Dealing with Unfamiliar Words

Fill in the blanks in the following sentences with the correct form of the words from the box.

optimize	lucid	dual	formulate	thriving
install	momentum	emission	combat	lush
implementation	manifest	mechanism	desertification	manufacturer

(1) If we continue to destroy forests, land _____ will be an inevitable result.

(2) Companies can also _____ their energy use and cut down on the cost of electricity.

(3) The _____ of gases such as carbon dioxide should be stabilized at their present level.

(4) Governments need to _____ energy policies that promote economically and environmentally sound development.

(5) The place has rapidly developed from a small fishing community into a _____ tourist resort.

(6) Our destination was a beautiful piece of land with _____ grasses, a small stream, and a forested foothill in the background.

(7) The economic market is a self-correcting _____, which does not need regulation by government.

(8) Cooperation between police forces and the art world is vital to _____ art crime.

(9) The football players began to lose _____ in the second half of the game.

(10) New York appears to _____ some of the best features of America.

2. Reading and Understanding

Decide whether the following statements are true (T) or false (F).

(1) The "dual carbon" goals are expected to be achieved at the same time.

(2) China has been trying to optimize its energy mix for many years.

(3) Carbon markets serve as accelerators for advancing climate action.

(4) Social economy and ecological environment cannot realize coordinated development.

(5) The world is watching how China completes the green transition and will learn from it.

3. Translating

Translate the following paragraph into Chinese.

As the world's second-largest economy and a global leader in renewable energy, China's green transition can benefit billions of people within and outside the country. No wonder many emerging economies are watching how this transition takes place in China. And this transition is central to the country's 14th Five-Year Plan (2021–2025). How well humans and nature coexist and thrive together depends on how well this transition is achieved.

4. Developing Critical Thinking

Work in pairs and discuss the following questions.

(1) Can you give some examples of how China is contributing to a greener planet?

(2) How did China manage to build a world-leading industry in electric vehicles?

Further Reading

China: from Follower to Leader in the Digital Economy

On December 22 at the 2021 World Digital Economy Forum, China officially released the "Jointly Building a Digital Community with a Shared Future Initiative," which captured worldwide attention. This initiative represents China's response to the complex international situation in the global digital economy. As a responsible power, China now provides a "blueprint" for the development of the digital economy reflecting a willingness to work together with countries around the world to build a healthy digital community and provide constructive solutions for governance of the internet economy.

In recent years, China's digital economy has developed rapidly and has gradually become one of the dominant forces in the national economy.

According to the global digital economy white paper released by the China Academy of Information and Communications Technology, China's digital economy in 2020 experienced strong growth, reaching 39.2 trillion yuan ($6.2 trillion), accounting for 38.6 percent of GDP, an increase of 2.4 percentage points from the previous year. The digital economy of China's service industry, manufacturing industry, and agriculture accounted for 40.7 percent, 21.0 percent, and 8.9 percent of the industry's added value, respectively. This also greatly contributed to the effective COVID-19 prevention and control measures as well as to stabilizing economic and social development.

Furthermore, the structure of the digital economy continued to be optimized and upgraded. According to the core digital industry statistical classification by the National Bureau of Statistics of China, China's digital economy is mainly driven by two segments: Firstly, industrialization of digital products and services and secondly, digitization of traditional industries. The scale of the industrialization of digital products and services has reached 7.5 trillion yuan ($1.2 trillion), accounting for 19.1 percent of the digital economy, 7.3 percent of GDP, and a nominal year-on-year increase of 5.3 percentage points.

More importantly, the digital transformation of traditional industry is also accelerating. The white paper shows the size of the economy generated by the digitization of traditional industry has reached 31.7 trillion yuan, accounting for 80.9 percent of the digital economy, 31.2 percent of GDP, and a nominal year-on-year increase of 10.3 percent, which provides strong impetus for the sustainable and healthy development of the digital economy.

The report also pointed out that in 2020, China's digital economy ranked second in the world, with nearly $5.4 trillion, behind the United States. In terms of growth rate, China's digital economy grew by 9.6 percent year-on-year, one of the highest in the world.

China has become an important source of innovation in the global digital economy. This means that the era of China as a "follower" is over, and it will gradually become a "leader".

China then will take the lead in entering the "uncharted waters" in the era of fierce competition in the formulation of international digital rules and accelerated reshaping of the international order in cyberspace. In the past 10 years, the world has seen China's new formats and models in the digital economy, such as e-commerce, mobile payment and bicycles sharing. More recently, in the past three years, China has made further advancements in information aggregation, data sharing and AI analytics, which have been applied to the fight against the COVID-19 epidemic, thus making it possible to allocate resources efficiently in the society, improve the normal flow of goods and develop remote office work.

Looking ahead, in the next 5 to 10 years China will not only inject a steady stream of vitality into the recovery and development of the world economy, but also will provide the world with a "Chinese example" and "Chinese plan" of digital economy innovation. In addition, China, as a major country, will also take on the responsibilities of actively participating in the formulation of international taxation rules and strengthening the formulation of international governance rules for the digital economy.

For China, this is a huge responsibility and challenge. According to the country's future digital economy plan, it will not only be necessary to further increase the scale of the country's digital economy development, but also do a good job in the role of a world leader. These are necessary goals to empower the transformation and upgrading of traditional industries, give birth to new industries, new business models, and new models for the world and at the same time enhance the service awareness of global business formats, facilitate win-win cooperation in the global digital economy and promote the solution of problems related to global digital economy governance.

In terms of creating a good environment, China needs to work with other countries on the basis of conscientiously summarizing practical experiences and strive to form a new global rule system that is practical and acceptable to everyone.

From the perspective of global governance, China should join forces with other countries to implement the five sectors mentioned in the "Jointly Building a Digital Community with a Shared Future Initiative": Firstly, global digital economic cooperation; secondly, global digital trade rules; thirdly, global digital economic development opportunities; fourthly, digital technology solutions; and fifthly, win-win digital innovation and development.

As to China's digital economy perspective, it needs to pay special attention to the following three points:

The first is necessary to focus on accelerating the deployment of China's digital economy in the service sector, especially in the IT and internet service industries such as artificial intelligence, big data, and cloud computing.

The second is to pay more attention to the development of international cooperation in the development of the digital economy, especially to promote the international development of the service sector of the digital economy.

The third is to closely follow the progress of the international reform of digital taxation, strengthen theoretical research and practical exploration of digital taxation, actively participate in the formulation of international taxation rules, and combine the development of the global digital economy to jointly build a standardized, fair, scientific, and reasonable digital tax system.

The digital economy has increasingly become the leading force to promote economic development. China is discussing with countries around the world and issued the "Jointly Building a Digital Community with a Shared Future Initiative" to create a more harmonious and win-win ecosystem for the development of the digital economy in the post-epidemic era. China will provide useful experience in its leading role for the development of digital industries around the world, join forces with all countries in the world and make active efforts and contributions to the governance of the global digital economy.

(Source: https://news.cgtn.com/news/2021-12-24/China-From-follower-to-leader-in-the-digital-economy-16fDlYMaMX6/index.html)

Unit 2

Chinese Modernization

Text A

China Forges Ahead on Chinese Path to Modernization

2023 is the first full year for implementing the guiding principles of the 20th National Congress of the Communist Party of China. Ahead of this year's Two Sessions, China's key annual political meetings, CGTN is publishing "China Marches On," a special series that takes an in-depth look at the country's endeavors in advancing Chinese modernization.

As one of the engines driving China's economic growth, Jiangsu Province holds great significance in constructing a Chinese path to modernization. The important features of Chinese modernization goals are widely and vividly reflected in Jiangsu.

In 2014, 2017 and 2020, Chinese President Xi Jinping inspected Jiangsu three times and drew a grand blueprint of a strong economy, affluent people, a beautiful environment and a highly civilized society for the province.

Since the 18th National Congress of the Communist Party of China (CPC), Xi has conducted in-depth inspections in Jiangsu's Zhenjiang, Nanjing, Xuzhou, Nantong and other places, and devoted a lot of efforts to the economic and social development of Jiangsu, a hot land of reform and opening-up.

Jiangsu under the New Development Pattern

China has been comprehensively pursuing modernization. It has coordinated material and cultural-ethical progress, promoted economic, political, cultural, social and ecological development, and adhered to a new development philosophy that highlights innovation, coordination, greenness, openness and sharing.

Jiangsu has always been at the forefront of modernization construction. In the past decade, Jiangsu continued advancing its construction and laid a solid foundation for striving to write a new chapter in the construction of modernization.

While inspecting Jiangsu in 2014, Xi said innovation-driven development must rely on realizing the sustainable and healthy growth of China's economy, adding that it is necessary to further promote the close integration of technology and the economy and increase the contribution of scientific and technological progress to economic growth.

In 2022, Jiangsu's GDP reached 12.28 trillion yuan ($1.77 trillion), a 2.8-percent increase over the previous year, and its economic output accounted for 10.2 percent of the country's total.

Jiangsu's foreign investment in actual use reached $30.5 billion in 2022, a year-on-year increase of 5.7 percent, ranking first in the country. The province approved an additional 35 regional headquarters and functional institutions of multi-national corporations, bringing the total to 366.

As the key to economic transformation and development is to apply the new development philosophy and follow a development path featuring increased productivity, prosperous life and a sound ecological environment, Jiangsu improves the modernization level of ecological and environmental governance and realizes the positive interaction between high-level protection and high-quality development.

The annual average concentration of PM2.5 in Jiangsu continued to fall in 2021, recording drops for eight consecutive years. The water quality of Taihu Lake has been the best in the past 10 years, and the water quality of the Jiangsu section of the Yangtze River is reaching an excellent level.

By implementing a 10-year fishing ban on the Yangtze River, Jiangsu has made solid progress in ecological conservation and promoted the high-quality development of the Yangtze River Economic Belt.

Overall, Jiangsu's prominent economic strength is leading China's economy striding forward in the new era, along with the high-quality development becoming a distinctive feature.

China on the Path to Common Prosperity

Chinese modernization is the modernization of over 1.4 billion people — a figure greater than the combined population of all developed countries in the world today.

While illustrating Chinese modernization at the opening of a study session at the Party School of the CPC Central Committee on February 7, Xi said it is the modernization of a huge population and common prosperity for all. Xi's remarks signaled the country's commitment to taking the people's aspirations, both at home and abroad, for a better life as the modernization's ultimate goal.

China has eliminated absolute poverty and realized its first centenary goal — building a moderately prosperous society in all respects.

Figures speak. China's total economic volume exceeded 120 trillion yuan in 2022, a new leap forward after breaking through 100 trillion yuan and 110 trillion yuan in 2020 and 2021.

The country's average GDP growth rate has been 6.6 percent over the past decade, and the total number of employed people in urban areas has increased from 370 million to 480 million, with an average annual increase of more than 13 million.

As a major engine driving the world's economic growth, China's economy is full of resilience and vitality, and has attracted worldwide attention.

China's contribution to global economic growth averaged 38.6 percent between 2013 and 2021, higher than the contributions of all Group of Seven countries combined.

In 2021, China's GDP accounted for 18.5 percent of the world's total economic output, an increase of 7.2 percentage points from 10 years ago. Meanwhile, the total trade volume in goods and services was $6.9 trillion, an increase of 56.8 percent from 10 years ago.

As Xi stressed, advancing Chinese modernization is a systematic endeavor, and it is also an exploratory undertaking.

"The cause of promoting Chinese modernization, which is an unprecedented and pioneering venture, will inevitably encounter all kinds of risks, challenges, difficulties and even dangerous storms, some of which we can foresee and others we cannot," Xi said. "Let us harness our indomitable fighting spirit to open new horizons for our cause."

(Source: https://news.cgtn.com/news/2023-02-26/China-forges-ahead-on-Chinese-path-to-modernization-1hJugUF6kKI/index.html)

Language Focus

Words and Expressions

endeavor *n.* 努力；尝试	an attempt to do something
blueprint *n.* 行动方案，规划，蓝图	an early plan or design that explains how something might be achieved
affluent *adj.* 富裕的，富足的	having a lot of money or owning a lot of things
coordinate *v.* 协调，配合	to make many different things work effectively as a whole

adhere to *phrv.* 坚持；遵守	to continue to behave according to a particular rule, agreement, or belief
headquarters *n.* 总部，总公司	the main offices of an organization such as the army, the police, or a business company
consecutive *adj.* 连续的，不间断的	(events, numbers, etc.) follow one after another without an interruption
prominent *adj.* 重要的，著名的	very well known and important
aspiration *n.* 渴望，抱负，志向	a strong desire to achieve things
resilience *n.* 恢复力，复原力	the ability to be happy, successful, etc. again after something difficult or bad has happened
vitality *n.* 活力，热情	energy and strength
venture *n.* 投机活动；商业冒险	a new activity, usually in business, that involves risk or uncertainty
inevitable *adj.* 必然发生的，不可避免的	certain to happen and unable to be avoided or prevented
indomitable *adj.* 不屈不挠的；不服输的；不气馁的	used to say that someone is strong, brave, determined, and difficult to defeat or frighten

Notes and Explanations

➢ The Yangtze River Economic Belt 长江经济带：东起长三角地区，西至云贵高原，覆盖上海、江苏、浙江、安徽、江西、湖北、湖南、四川、重庆、云南、贵州等11个省（市），包括中国农业、工业、商业、文化教育和科学技术等方面最发达的地区，也连接着中国十分贫困的地区。

➢ Group of Seven 七国集团：成员国包括美国、英国、法国、德国、日本、意大利和加拿大7个国家。

➢ PM2.5 PM2.5值：也称细颗粒物，英文全称为2.5-micrometer particulate matter。指环境空气中空气动力学当量直径小于等于2.5微米的颗粒物。它能较长时间悬浮于空气中，其在空气中含量浓度越高，就代表空气污染越严重。

> Taihu Lake 太湖：位于江苏省南部，是中国五大淡水湖之一，湖泊面积2427.8平方千米。太湖河港纵横，河口众多，有主要进出河流50余条。太湖岛屿众多，有50多个，其中18个岛屿有人居住。

Exercises

1. Dealing with Unfamiliar Words
   Match the words in the left with their definitions.

   (1) endeavor   energy and strength

   (2) aspiration   a new activity, usually in business, that involves risk or uncertainty

   (3) headquarters an early plan or design that explains how something might be achieved

   (4) blueprint   a strong desire to achieve things

   (5) resilience   the ability to be happy, successful, etc. again after something difficult

   (6) venture   an attempt to do something

   (7) vitality   the main offices of an organization, e.g., the police, or a business company

   (8) coordinate   organize the different parts of an activity and the people involved in it

2. Reading and Understanding
   Decide whether the following statements are true (T) or false (F).

   (1) According to President Xi, Chinese modernization aims to provide common prosperity for all Chinese people.

   (2) China's development philosophy has not changed since 1978.

   (3) According to figures, the total economic volume of China saw an upward trend in 2022.

   (4) Jiangsu has implemented the philosophy of new development in its modernization process.

   (5) China has eliminated absolute poverty and realized its first centenary goal — achieving common prosperity for all.

3. Questions for Discussion
   Work in small groups and discuss the following questions.

   (1) What development experience can other provinces learn from Jiangsu Province?

   (2) In your imagination, what is it like when common prosperity is achieved for all Chinese people?

   (3) Why is the indomitable fighting spirit important? How can you apply it in your life?

4. Translating

Translate the following paragraph into English.

中国式现代化，是中国共产党领导的社会主义现代化。中国式现代化基于中国实践，又同世界大势高度契合，是走和平发展道路、人与自然和谐共生的现代化，将为中国同世界各国合作提供新的机遇。中国式现代化既有各国现代化的共同特征，更有基于自己国情的中国特色。

Text B

China's Modernization Promotes Global Peace and Development

Noting that 2023 is the first year for fully implementing the guiding principles from the 20th National Congress of the Communist Party of China, the approaching "Two Sessions" will grab the world's attention. To better understand China's development blueprint, CGTN has curated the "Towards China's Modernization" series, and this is the first piece. Christopher Helali is the international secretary of the Party of Communists USA and a PhD candidate in philosophy and China Government Scholar for Sino-U.S. Cultural Communication at Tongji University. The article reflects the author's opinions and not necessarily the views of CGTN.

The 20th National Congress of the Communist Party of China (CPC) which was held in October 2022, outlined for the first time the necessity of Chinese modernization. On the path to China's rejuvenation, the modernization of the Chinese nation is critical to ensuring prosperity, stability, and peace.

Chinese President Xi Jinping said Chinese modernization is not only for China but for the world. That is, China's modernization and ongoing development does not merely lift the Chinese people's living standards and their prosperity, but also raises global prosperity. In a dialectical relationship, Chinese prosperity is tied to the prosperity of the world. If China prospers, the world prospers and vice-versa.

For centuries, the Chinese have endured barbarities, injustices, and plundering of their national resources under the yoke of colonialism. Today, the Chinese stand tall and proud. No longer will the Chinese nation submit to outside meddling of their internal affairs. No longer will the natural resources and wealth of the Chinese get plundered by imperialist powers.

The Chinese path to modernization is born out of the wisdom accumulated from a long history of struggle and sacrifice. This was reflected in the 20th National Congress of the CPC, as well as the documents and policies that have emerged from it.

The Communist Party of China under the leadership of General Secretary of the CPC Central Committee Xi Jinping is committed to realizing socialist modernization in all respects. That means, building China into a strong, prosperous, democratic, harmonious, technologically advanced, and ecologically sustainable society over the next few decades.

Over the past few years, China's alleviation of extreme poverty has shown the world its commitment of the CPC to bringing prosperity to all Chinese. This victory proves China's dedication to a people-centered philosophy, which is rooted in socialism with Chinese characteristics.

China's economy has become the main engine that powers the global economy. In 2022, the Chinese economy's volume was over 120 trillion yuan ($17.39 trillion), a new record. The country's GDP is growing and wages and conditions continue to rise across the board.

Moreover, China's modernization has broad impacts in other fields including in science and technology. China has proven to be a leading force in cutting edge space technology, launching its own satellites, crewed missions, and building its own space station. China's commitment to human advancement extends far beyond our planet as the Chinese nation pursues peaceful exploration of the moon, mars, and beyond.

China's modernization utilizes the power of the Chinese economy to peacefully develop economies throughout the developing world. Unlike imperialist powers in the West, China uses its economy not for war but for peace. It achieves this with a win-win strategy in mind, not a strategy of hegemony and neocolonialism.

Chinese projects such as the Belt and Road Initiative (BRI) would invest in countries across the world and build bridges and links to both people and economies. This along with other initiatives like the Global Development Initiative (GDI), the Global Security Initiative (GSI), and institutions including BRICS seek to usher in a multipolar world, ending decades of U.S. dollar hegemony and Western economic monopolies. Chinese modernization is committed to the peace and prosperity for all.

In just two decades, China has built a modern rail system linking many parts of the country with technologically advanced trains and infrastructure, capable of moving millions of people daily at high speeds. Every time I visit China, I marvel at all the efficient trains and investment in infrastructure and technology.

In stark contrast, the recent train disaster in East Palestine, Ohio revealed the decay of infrastructure in the U.S. I, as an American, am appalled by trains and subway systems in the U.S., especially in New York City and Boston, the home to renowned institutions including Harvard and MIT.

Advancing a socialist culture to foster the ideals, which have liberated and constructed China into a cornerstone of Chinese modernization. The intangible cultural heritage of the Chinese nation is a treasure for the world. For more than 5,000 years Chinese civilization has made countless advancements in philosophy, science, technology, art, poetry, language, and medicine. Additionally, China has 56 cultural and natural UNESCO world heritage sites, second only to Italy.

China's modernization impacts more than 1.4 billion people, nearly 20 percent of the world's population. What happens in China also has enormous consequences for the rest of the world. While the military-industrial complex in the West continues to finance death, Chinese modernization is rooted in a people-centered philosophy geared towards the well-being and prosperity of all people. The CPC has made China's modernization a pivotal part of China's path to socialism in order to generate prosperity and peace for China and the world.

(Source: https://news.cgtn.com/news/2023-03-01/China-s-modernization-promotes-global-peace-and-development--1hOWf2rVzW0/index.html)

Language Focus

Words and Expressions

rejuvenation *n.* 恢复活力；复兴	the act or process of making an organization or system more effective by introducing new methods, ideas, or people
dialectical *adj.* 辩证的；辩证法的	a way of discovering what is true by considering opposite theories
plunder *v.* 掠夺，抢劫	to steal goods violently from a place, especially during a war
meddle *v.* 干涉；管闲事	to try to change or have an influence on things that are not your responsibility, especially by criticizing in a damaging or annoying way
alleviation *n.* 减轻，缓和	the act of making something bad such as pain or problems less severe
multipolar *adj.* （世界局势）多极的	involving several countries having most of the power
stark *adj.* 明显的，鲜明的	very different to something in a way that is easy to see
appalled *adj.* 惊骇的；反感的	having strong feelings of shock or disapproval
renown *n.* 名誉，声望	the state of being famous

foster v.　　　　　to promote the growth or development of
促进，培养

pivotal adj.　　　 central and important
中枢的，关键的

Notes and Explanations

➢ win-win strategy 双赢策略：一种在谈判或合作中寻求实现各方利益最大化的策略，使各方都能从中获益。

➢ BRICS 金砖国家：该词引用了巴西（Brazil）、俄罗斯（Russia）、印度（India）、中国（China）和南非（South Africa）的英文首字母且与砖（brick）的英语单词类似，因此被称为"金砖国家"。金砖国家国土面积占世界领土总面积的26.46%，人口占世界总人口的41.93%。

➢ Two Sessions 两会：对自1959年以来历年召开的中华人民共和国全国人民代表大会和中国人民政治协商会议的统称。由于两场会议会期基本重合，而且对于国家运作的重要程度都非常高，故简称"两会"。

➢ UNESCO 联合国教育、科学及文化组织：简称"联合国教科文组织"，英文全称为United Nations Educational, Scientific and Cultural Organization，成立于1945年11月16日，总部设于法国巴黎，现有194个成员和12个准成员。联合国教科文组织致力于推动各国在教育、科学和文化领域开展国际合作，以此共筑和平。

Exercises

1. Dealing with Unfamiliar Words

Fill in the blanks in the following sentences with the correct form of the words from the box.

usher	multipolar	alleviation	appalled	rejuvenation
dedication	pivot	meddle	renown	dialectic
stark	foster	mar	plunder	yoke

(1) It is a tradition round which this country's reputation and _____ have been wreathed with laurels for decades.

(2) Some believe that a _____ system leads to more flexible and stable relationships in international politics.

(3) Acupuncture might help with the _____ of headaches and migraines.

(4) But it also established a sort of _____ between centre and periphery, which was geographical rather than political or sociological.

(5) The idea of transcending our human failings through the purity and strength of _____, rebirth or resurrection has been etched in the consciousness of many cultures for millennia.

(6) With a certain amount of _____ and determination, you can achieve a great deal.

(7) It was harder for Bush to _____ to the positive when so much of his campaign revolved around taking down Kerry.

(8) She was _____ to see how much damage the storm had caused.

(9) A lawsuit is being launched against him claiming that he and his associates have _____ more than $300m from the company over the years.

(10) What is clear, however, is that decentralization _____ in a new form of uneven development.

2. Reading and Understanding

Decide whether the following statements are true (T) or false (F).

(1) The necessity of Chinese modernization has been proposed long before the 20th National Congress of CPC.

(2) Not only does China's modernization aim to improve wellbeing of Chinese people, but also people around the globe.

(3) Chinese prosperity and the prosperity of world complement each other.

(4) Due to the COVID-19 pandemic, Chinese economy's volume fell in 2022.

(5) Imperialistic western countries use economy as a weapon for war.

3. Translating

Translate the following paragraph into Chinese.

Moreover, China's modernization has broad impacts in other fields including in science and technology. China has proven to be a leading force in cutting edge space technology, launching its own satellites, crewed missions, and building its own space station. China's commitment to human advancement extends far beyond our planet as the Chinese nation pursues peaceful exploration of the moon, mars, and beyond.

4. Developing Critical Thinking

Work in pairs and discuss the following questions.

(1) In your opinion, what is China's greatest commitment to the world?

(2) Demonstrate "people-centered philosophy" in your own words, and explain why it is important for China.

Further Reading

Nation's Modernization Drive Attracts Global Attention

Shanghai Forum Participants Salute New Model for Human Advancement

As China strives to advance its modernization, international attention is focusing on how the nation will fulfill its ambition to become a modern socialist country by the middle of this century and how that process will affect the rest of the world.

The Communist Party of China (CPC) laid out the central task of advancing national rejuvenation through a Chinese path toward modernization at its 20th National Congress in October.

The Party views Chinese modernization as not being solely related to achieving material wealth or a higher level of efficiency than that offered by the capitalist system. Rather, it is about effectively maintaining a higher degree of social equity, providing 1.4 billion people with a prosperous and dignified life, and promoting harmony between humankind and nature.

More important, the CPC pledged that Chinese modernization will lay a path for peaceful development, and that China will not achieve modernization through colonization or invasion. Neither will it seek hegemony or expansion.

In a congratulatory message sent to the Lanting Forum on Chinese Modernization and the World, held in Shanghai on April 21, President Xi Jinping assured the world that China will provide new opportunities for global development with new accomplishments in Chinese modernization.

It will also give new impetus to humanity's search for paths toward modernization and better social systems.

Xi's comments were echoed by political leaders, business executives and think tank researchers from nearly 80 countries taking part in the forum. They said China's modernization not only matters to the well-being of the Chinese people, but also creates a new model for human advancement.

Dilma Rousseff, president of the New Development Bank, said: "As a former president of Brazil, I am fully aware of what different patterns of modernization can mean for the peoples of the Global South. Over the centuries, a false modernization was imposed on us, which initially took the form of colonialism, with its killings of the indigenous population, slavery and predatory extractivism."

Rousseff said that more recently, financial neo-liberalism has implied a brutal process of concentration of income and wealth in the hands of a few, and once again, millions of people have been left behind.

"The push for modernization proposed and promoted by China provides a new choice and demonstrates that another world is necessary and possible. This is crucial at this time of greater fragmentation caused by climate change, by the intensification of geopolitical conflicts, by the disruption of production chains, and by a movement of de-globalization," she said.

Rousseff commended the Chinese path toward modernization, particularly its principle of promoting common prosperity.

"The great effect of this modernization for countries of the Global South lies in building a community with a shared future for mankind. And this commitment made by China could help bridge the gap between the global North and South and help create a more inclusive multipolar international order," she said.

Tough Journey

Modernization for China has been a journey of hardship and perseverance. In modern times, countless Chinese patriots have looked to the West for a modernization formula to save the nation, but all the formulas failed.

Under the leadership of the CPC, China has found a path to modernization through its own efforts. Over the past 100 years or so, the nation has transformed from being impoverished and backward into the world's second-largest economy, the top trader in goods, the biggest holder of foreign exchange reserves, and the biggest manufacturer.

China has put in place the world's largest compulsory education system, social security system, and medical and health system — achieving in just a few decades industrialization that took developed countries several centuries to realize.

Over the 40-plus years since reform and opening-up was launched, the Chinese government has lifted more than 800 million people out of poverty and increased the middle-income group's population to over 400 million.

China is now the main trading partner of more than 140 countries and regions. It places $320 million in direct investment around the world each day, while attracting over 3,000 foreign businesses every month, Foreign Ministry data show. Over the past decade, China has contributed more to global growth than all the G7 countries combined.

Foreign investors cannot afford to ignore the immense commercial prospects created by the vast Chinese market that boasts a rapidly growing middle-income group. Due to uncertainty caused by mounting geopolitical competition between major countries, some observers may be skeptical about China's modernization process, but others consider it has enormous potential.

Martin Jacques, former senior fellow at Cambridge University's Department of Politics and International Studies, said that when it comes to the nature of modernization, people always think of it primarily in technological and economic terms.

"I think that is obviously important, but it's much too narrow, because fundamental to Western modernization was the division of the world. Fundamental to Chinese modernization are only the opportunities to the world, particularly to the developing world, to develop and to modernize," he said.

Jacques added that Western modernization started at a time when Western countries used the rest of the world as a way to enrich themselves. In an extraordinary shift, the developing world had its first opportunity to modernize in the second half of the 20th century, he said.

"Led ultimately by China, you get this incredible transformation where modernization is actually the possibility for all of humanity, not for a tiny minority of Western countries. So the arrival of the developing world and the arrival of China transform the whole global landscape."

Noting that China's growth is redefining the notion of modernization, Jacques said the nation's rise is going to change the world in a way the West can't cope with. "The West, in my view, is basically frozen. It has no strategy. It doesn't understand China. It's like a rabbit caught in the headlights," he said.

Strategic Plan

To build itself into a great modern socialist country in all respects, China has adopted a two-step strategic plan — to basically realize socialist modernization from 2020 through 2035, and to become a great modern socialist country that is prosperous, strong, democratic, culturally advanced, harmonious and beautiful from 2035 through the middle of this century.

Xi, who is also general secretary of the CPC Central Committee, said at the 20th CPC National Congress: "In pursuing modernization, China will not tread the old path of war, colonization and plunder taken by some countries... We will strive to safeguard world peace and development as we pursue our own development, and we will make greater contributions to world peace and development through our own development."

Observers said the Chinese path toward modernization abandons the old Western way of modernization, which is capital-centric and characterized by soaring materialism and external expansion. It also breaks the myth that modernization means westernization, and expands choices for developing countries on their modernization journey.

Essam Sharaf, former Egyptian prime minister and a non-resident senior fellow at Renmin University of China's Chongyang Institute for Financial Studies, said he sees four key pillars in Chinese modernization — cooperation, harmony, peace and development.

He said that by adopting these pillars, China passes on the benefits of its modernization to the world through the Belt and Road Initiative(BRI), the Global Development

Initiative (GDI), the Global Security Initiative (GSI) and the Global Civilization Initiative (GCI), which are considered public goods offered by the nation to the international community.

Mamadou Tangara, Gambia's foreign minister, said China's modernization "addresses, in a resolute way, the global deficits of development, peace, governance and trust."

China's rapid economic growth and long-term social stability are widely viewed as a miracle in the history of human development, Tanggara said, and the nation has promoted poverty alleviation, common prosperity, ecological conservation and people-centered democracy as well as the rule of law.

"China has inspired many developing countries to seek their own formula to reduce poverty and to promote their respective economic development and prosperity," he said.

Tangara described the BRI, as an effective platform to promote a more integrated world where "positive collaboration between countries is not burdened by the complexities of ideological and cultural differences."

"Under the BRI, we are all galvanized under the common ambition of seeking mutually beneficial and sustainable socioeconomic transformative partnerships. It essentially bridges physical distance and shared interests and prosperity," he said.

Tangara also voiced his support for the GDI, the GSI and the GCI, saying they unwaveringly offer hope for a shared and better future for humankind.

Since China proposed the BRI in 2013, more than 3,000 cooperation projects have been launched, involving investment of nearly $1 trillion and creating 420,000 jobs for participating countries, the Foreign Ministry said. As a result, many nations have realized their dreams of building railways and large bridges, and also of alleviating poverty.

The GDI has been widely welcomed by the international community. With the support of more than 100 countries and many international organizations, and with some 70 countries in the Group of Friends of the GDI, the initiative is giving a strong boost to the early attainment of the UN Sustainable Development Goals for 2030.

John Thornton, co-chair of the Board of Trustees of the Asia Society in the United States, said: "The concept of Chinese modernization, to me, is very compelling. It is enduring. It is inspiring. And I see it as kind of an aspiration and also a guide to behavior."

He suggests that the single most important thing for Chinese modernization is to figure out how to communicate the content in a compelling way through global communication channels so that everybody hears the same message.

"Who in the world is not in favor of peace? Who in the world is not in favor of common prosperity? Who in the world is not in favor of harmony between man and nature?" he said.

"And if at least in my country, if people understood that this is what China believes, this is what they stand for, this is where they see the future, then that will have a very positive impact on the relationship between the two countries."

Challenges Ahead

While striving to advance Chinese modernization, the CPC is keeping a cool head about the risks and challenges that lie ahead. "Building a modern socialist country in all respects is a great and arduous endeavor," Xi said at the 20th CPC National Congress.

Analyzing the international situation, he said momentous changes unseen in a century are accelerating across the world, the once-in-a-century pandemic has had far-reaching effects, global economic recovery is sluggish, unilateralism and protectionism are mounting, regional conflicts and disturbances are frequent, and the world has entered a new period of turbulence and change.

At home, China faces many deep-seated problems regarding reform, development and stability. "In our efforts to strengthen the Party, and especially to improve conduct, build integrity, and combat corruption, we are confronted with many stubborn and recurrent problems. External attempts to suppress and contain China may escalate at any time," Xi said.

Amid new challenges arising from domestic and international situations, the CPC launched an education campaign last month to study and implement Xi Jinping Thought on Socialism with Chinese Characteristics for a New Era, with a view to building consensus among all its members to make united efforts to advance Chinese modernization for national rejuvenation.

As part of the theoretical study program, the Party launched a research and fact-finding drive aimed at solving new practical problems and serving scientific decision-making.

(Source: http://www.chinadaily.com.cn/a/202305/10/WS645ad2dea310b6054fad2018.html)

Unit 3

China's Science and Technology

Text A

What Does China's Innovation-Driven Development Strategy Mean for the World?

From the Yutu-2 lunar rover roaming on the "dark side" of the moon to the Fendouzhe submersible exploring the 10,000-meter deep ocean, and from salt-tolerant rice growing in tidal flats near the sea to Chinese unmanned equipment guided by the Beidou Navigation Satellite System to help African farmers boost crop yields... the saga of China's sci-tech innovation continues to unfold.

During the ongoing "two sessions," Chinese President Xi Jinping emphasized the imperative to accelerate the implementation of the innovation-driven development strategy, saying that speeding up efforts to achieve greater self-reliance and strength in science and technology is the path China must take to advance high-quality development.

Over 10 years into the nation's innovation-driven development strategy, China saw its ranking in the Global Innovation Index jump from 34th in 2012 to 11th last year, with the economy expanding at an average annual rate of 6.6 percent between 2013 and 2021, contributing over 30 percent to world economic growth.

When reinforcing its strength in science and technology, the country has also been committed to sharing its technology with worldwide partners and cooperating to improve global science and technology governance.

Innovation-Driven Development

"The close attention paid by the government and the country to innovation as an engine of growth is paying off," said Daren Tang, director general of the World Intellectual Property Organization.

Indeed, China's historic progress in building an innovative country attests to the judgment: science and technology are the primary productive force, talent the primary resource and innovation the primary driver of growth.

The innovation-driven development strategy put forward at the 18th National Congress of the Communist Party of China has led China to join the ranks of the world's innovators, with success on various fronts over the past decade.

The country has expanded its research and development (R&D) expenditure from 1 trillion yuan (about 145 billion U.S. dollars) to 3.09 trillion yuan (about 445 billion U.S. dollars) in the past decade, the second highest in the world, with its R&D intensity rising from 1.91 percent to 2.55 percent, according to Ministry of Science and Technology.

Furthermore, China has coordinated its innovation blueprint with its strategy for invigorating China through science and education, which underscores development based on progress in science and technology and the workforce development strategy focusing on fostering high-quality talent. Now the country has become home to the largest cohort of R&D personnel around the globe.

Apart from calling for moving faster toward self-reliance in science and technology, Xi in late January pledged more efforts to ensure better allocation of innovation-related resources to make the country a global pacesetter in major sci-tech areas and a pioneer in advanced interdisciplinary fields, and ensure that China will become a major world hub for science and innovation as soon as possible.

Global Public Goods

The implications of China's innovation-driven development extend beyond its borders.

Boasting the world's longest and most extensively used high-speed rail network, China has been helping multiple countries construct and upgrade their rail transit with its advanced railway technology.

World Bank Vice President for South Asia Martin Raiser said China's rail technology would bring urban development, tourism and regional economic growth.

Take the China-Laos Railway, a landmark Belt and Road project. Since operations began in December 2021, landlocked Laos has become a land-linked hub in Southeast Asia. The railway's Lao section has created more than 110,000 local jobs.

Through multilateral mechanisms such as the Belt and Road Initiative and the Regional Comprehensive Economic Partnership, China's sci-tech achievements have delivered new options in 5G communications, biomedicine and numerous realms, while also providing growth momentum.

Gu Qingyang, a scholar at the National University of Singapore, said the extensive application of China's sci-tech accomplishments not only leads to its domestic industrial upgrading, but also lends impetus to the neighboring areas.

Similarly, at the World Economic Forum Annual Meeting 2023 earlier this year, Saadia

Zahidi, the forum's managing director, said, "when it comes to technology and innovation, much of what is being developed in China will change the world."

Given the size of its economy, China will help boost worldwide growth and inject optimism in the medium and long term, Zahidi told Xinhua.

Global Sci-Tech Governance

China would never innovate behind closed doors. That's why the country has been dedicated to advancing global governance in science and technology.

In late February, Xi restated his call for promoting the openness, trust and cooperation of the international science and technology community and making new and more significant contributions to the progress of human civilization.

Over recent years, China has adopted various policy tools to promote global sci-tech cooperation, opened up large-scale scientific infrastructure, jointly established R&D platforms and expanded the scope, field and scale of open innovation.

In a typical example, China has advocated expanding international cooperation in the space sector. Romanian astronaut Dumitru Prunariu said China "actually invited all countries to perform scientific experiments" on its Tiangong space station. In addition, the country also welcomes broader collaboration in deep space exploration.

China has engaged in sci-tech cooperation with more than 160 countries and regions, participating in global science projects such as the International Thermonuclear Experimental Reactor program — one of the most ambitious energy projects in the world and the Square Kilometre Array — an intergovernmental radio telescope project.

Meanwhile, the country's accelerated transition from "Made in China" to "Created in China" shows the developing world how to uncover a development path suited to their own conditions.

China's experience in education, scientific research and technology is "inspiring" to Arab countries, Mohamed Abdel-Fattah Moustafa, head of the Arab Union for Education and Scientific Research, told Xinhua.

Its cooperation with other developing countries in education, scientific research and technology localization will help "create a new international community based on cooperation, exchange of benefits and mutual win," he said.

(Source: http://english.scio.gov.cn/in-depth/2023-03/10/content_85158296.htm)

Language Focus

Words and Expressions

navigate v. 导航，引路	to direct the way that a ship, aircraft, etc. will travel, or to find a direction across, along, or over an area of water or land, often by using a map
imperative adj. 极重要的，迫切的； 命令的，强制的	extremely important or urgent
attest v. 证明，表明	to show, say, or prove that something exists or is true
invigorating adj. 使精力充沛的，使生机勃勃的	making somebody feel healthier, less tired, and more energetic
cohort n. (有共同特点或举止类同的) 一群人，一批人；同伙，支持者	a group of people who share a characteristic, usually age
allocate v. 分配，分派	to give something to someone as their share of a total amount, to use in a particular way
hub n. (活动的) 中心；枢纽	the central or main part of something where there is most activity
implication n. 可能的影响（或作用、结果）	the effect that an action or decision will have on something else in the future
extensive adj. 广阔的；广泛的	covering a large area; having a great range
landmark n. 地标	a building or place that is easily recognized, especially one that you can use to judge where you are
impetus n. 动力	something that encourages a particular activity or makes that activity more energetic or effective

Notes and Explanations

➢ Yutu-2 lunar rover 玉兔二号：中国研制的嫦娥四号任务月球车（巡视器）。
➢ Beidou Navigation Satellite System 北斗卫星导航系统：中国自行研制的全球卫星导航系统，是世界上第三个成熟的卫星导航系统。
➢ World Intellectual Property Organization（WIPO）世界知识产权组织：联合国保护知识产权的一个专门机构，中国于1980年6月3日加入该组织。

Exercises

1. Dealing with Unfamiliar Words

   Match the words in the left with their definitions.

   (1) cohort   a group of people who share a characteristic, usually age

   (2) implication   a building or place that you can use to judge where you are

   (3) allocate   the effect that an action or decision will have on something else in the future

   (4) impetus   a change from one type to another, or the process by which this happens

   (5) transition   something that encourages a particular activity

   (6) hub   the central or main part of something where there is most activity

   (7) landmark   to give something to someone as their share of a total amount

   (8) navigation   the skill or the process of planning a route for a ship or other vehicle and taking it there

2. Reading and Understanding

   Decide whether the following statements are true (T) or false (F).

   (1) According to President Xi, China has to achieve independence in science and technology.

   (2) Since 2012, the Global Innovation Index has seen an upward trend.

   (3) Chinese government has put huge investment to innovation and gained great benefits from it.

   (4) Asserting a limited effect, China's innovation-driven development only contributes to its domestic economy.

   (5) "Created in China" is a more suitable development path for China now.

3. Questions for Discussion

Work in small groups and discuss the following questions.

(1) What has China achieved in innovation?

(2) To implement innovation blueprint, what can China do?

(3) How does China's innovation-driven development extend beyond its borders?

4. Translating

Translate the following paragraph into English.

传统制造业是现代化产业体系的基底,要加快数字化转型,推广先进适用技术,着力提升高端化、智能化、绿色化水平。要加快新能源、人工智能、生物制造、绿色低碳、量子计算等前沿技术研发和应用推广,支持专精特新企业发展。

Unit 3 China's Science and Technology

Text B

China Pursues Self-Reliant Sci-Tech Progress to Benefit All

Thousands of national legislators and political advisors are in Beijing for annual sessions that will set key development agenda of China for the year and beyond. Achieving self-reliance and self-improvement in science and technology has been a heatedly discussed topic as the country aims for high-quality development driven by innovation.

Not far from the main venue of the sessions, the Great Hall of the People, a popular exhibition is being staged at the National Museum of China to showcase the progress of the country's manned space program over 30 years, precisely illustrating how China has accomplished in sci-tech self-reliance as well as benefits it has brought to the world.

Self-Reliant but Open

According to a government work report submitted Sunday for the national legislators to deliberate, breakthroughs have been made in core technologies in key fields, and a series of innovations have emerged in areas such as manned spaceflight, lunar and Martian exploration, deep-sea and deep-earth probes, supercomputers, satellite navigation, quantum information, nuclear power technology, airliner manufacturing and artificial intelligence.

In late 2022, China's space station Tiangong entered the new phase of application and development. It now features a basic three-module configuration consisting of the core module named Tianhe, and two lab modules, Wentian and Mengtian.

The construction of the space station benefits from China's system of pooling national resources and strengths. Hundreds of thousands of scientific researchers have participated in the program, inspired by the spirit of self-reliance and independent innovation. The self-development rate of key components of the space station reached 100 percent.

Chinese President Xi Jinping has stressed on many occasions the importance of self-reliance and self-improvement in science and technology. Speeding up efforts to achieve greater self-reliance and strength in science and technology is the path China must take to advance high-quality development, said Xi, also general secretary of the Communist Party of China (CPC) Central Committee and chairman of the Central Military Commission, while attending a deliberation with his fellow deputies from the delegation of Jiangsu Province on Sunday at the ongoing first session of the 14th National People's Congress (NPC), China's national legislature.

To open up new areas and new arenas in development and foster new growth drivers and new strengths in face of fierce international competition, China should ultimately rely on scientific and technological innovation, he said.

Building self-reliance and strength in science and technology is key to building China into a great modern socialist country in all respects within the set time frame, Xi added.

The nation's achievements in space exploration, with the space station construction as an outstanding example, reflect the strength of innovation in China, said Wang Xiaojun, head of the China Academy of Launch Vehicle Technology and a member of the 14th National Committee of the Chinese People's Political Consultative Conference, the top political advisory body.

Sci-tech empowerment is a prominent symbol of China's high-quality development, while sci-tech innovation has become an important driving force for Chinese modernization, Wang added.

The country moved up to the 11th place in the 2022 Global Innovation Index and firmly remains the only middle-income economy in the top 30, according to the latest ranking published by the World Intellectual Property Organization.

China's spending on research and development totaled 3.09 trillion yuan (about 445 billion U.S. dollars) in 2022, an increase of 10.4 percent over the previous year, according to the National Bureau of Statistics.

Not only does the perseverance with self-reliance advance the sci-tech development of China, but it also creates more opportunities for global cooperation.

In its manned space program, China has signed agreements and carried out cooperation projects with France, Germany, Italy, Russia, Pakistan, and many space agencies and organizations. Its Tiangong space station is the first of its kind open to all UN member states.

In a cooperation program with the United Nations Office for Outer Space Affairs, projects from 17 countries have been included in the first batch of Tiangong's experiments in aerospace medicine, life sciences and biotechnology, microgravity physics and combustion science, astronomy and other emerging technologies.

China is fully aware that independent innovation should never exclude international cooperation.

The Global Chain

Self-reliance in science and technology has helped Chinese high-tech enterprises to forge their core competitiveness, and enabled them to become an essential part in the global innovative industrial chain.

Located in Ningde, east China's Fujian Province, battery producer Contemporary Amperex Technology Co., Limited (CATL) is now operating at full capacity, with its blue battery cells to be shipped to automakers worldwide, including BMW, Tesla, Mercedes-

Benz, Volkswagen and Volvo. Founded in 2011, CATL has ranked first in the world in terms of the usage of its power battery system for six consecutive years, and also in the shipment of its energy storage battery for two consecutive years.

To get more deeply involved in global industrial cooperation, CATL has built power battery production plants in Thuringia of Germany and Debrecen of Hungary. In February, it confirmed that it would work with Ford Motor Company on the latter's lithium iron phosphate battery plant in the U.S. state of Michigan, providing technology and service support to the new plant.

In 2022, China's foreign trade withstood the impact of multiple unexpected factors, with exports of EVs, photovoltaic (PV) products and lithium batteries growing by 131.8 percent, 67.8 percent and 86.7 percent, respectively.

According to the China Photovoltaic Industry Association, China's global market share of PV polysilicon, lithium battery cells and modules exceeded 70 percent in 2021.

"China today is the biggest driver of clean energy technologies," Fatih Birol, chief of the International Energy Agency, said at the World Economic Forum in Davos in January.

Zou Ming, an NPC deputy and a senior engineer with the Panzhihua Iron and Steel Research Institute, said that enterprises should give full play to the major role of innovation and transform sci-tech innovation into the biggest driving force on the Chinese path to modernization.

Benefits for All

While adhering to independent innovation, China has been actively promoting sci-tech sharing and exchanges, aiming to benefit all mankind.

The contribution of scientific and technological progress to the country's economic growth has exceeded 60 percent, said the government work report.

In February, a group of guests from Mexico came to Fujian Province to study the technology of "Juncao," an economical and environmentally friendly substitute for timber as a substrate for growing mushrooms.

Discovered by Chinese scientists, Juncao is famed as "magic grass," as it is particularly suitable for developing countries to improve their agriculture and reduce poverty.

It is becoming a new sustainable industry in countries and regions along the Belt and Road and has been introduced to 106 countries, creating hundreds of thousands of job opportunities and helping to alleviate poverty.

At a UN meeting in 2019, former President of the General Assembly Maria Fernanda Espinosa Garces described Juncao as "emblematic of China's Belt and Road Initiative," which, according to the World Bank's estimates, could contribute to lifting 7.6 million people out of extreme poverty and 32 million out of moderate poverty.

China has also hosted a large number of international students learning about the Juncao technology. So far, the country has held 310 international training sessions on the technology, both at home and abroad, training more than 10,000 people.

When chairing a group study session of the Political Bureau of the CPC Central Committee last month, Xi noted that efforts should be made to enhance openness, trust and cooperation in the international sci-tech community to make new and greater contributions to the progress of human civilization.

China has established sci-tech cooperation relations with more than 160 countries and regions, and signed 116 inter-governmental agreements on sci-tech cooperation. In 2022, China signed or renewed 25 international sci-tech cooperation documents, and carried out fruitful cooperation with many countries in multiple fields, including COVID-19 control, biodiversity, climate change and clean energy.

The country's Five-hundred-meter Aperture Spherical Radio Telescope has been available for scientists worldwide since April 1, 2021. Meanwhile, products, technologies and services related to the Beidou Navigation Satellite System have been applied in more than half of all countries around the world.

After the recent devastating earthquake hit Türkiye, China quickly deployed several satellites to help analyze the disaster situation and allocate relief resources. Sci-tech progress will make China better prepared for international sci-tech cooperation, and the country will continue to contribute to global sci-tech development for the benefit of humanity.

(Source: http://english.scio.gov.cn/in-depth/2023-03/07/content_85149685.htm)

Language Focus

Words and Expressions

legislate v. 立法，制定法律	to make or enact laws
deliberate v. 慎重考虑；审议，商议	think about carefully; weigh; discuss the pros and cons of an issue
manufacture v. 制造；生产	to make goods or wares by manual labor or by machinery, especially on a large scale
configure v. 配置，设置	to set up for a particular purpose

commission *n.* 委员会		a special group delegated to consider some matter
delegation *n.* 代表团		the body of delegates chosen to represent a political unit, as a state, in an assembly
forge *v.* 打造;形成		to develop something new, especially a strong relationship with other people, groups, or countries
deputy *n.* 代表;代理		a person appointed to represent or act on behalf of others
deploy *v.* 部署		to distribute systematically or strategically

Notes and Explanations

➢ Tiangong "天宫": 中国空间站的名称,是一个长期在近地轨道运行的国家级太空实验室。"天宫"由天和核心舱、问天实验舱、梦天实验舱组成,提供三个对接口,支持载人飞船、货运飞船及其他来访航天器的对接和停靠。它运行在高度400～450千米的近圆轨道,约每90分钟绕地球一周。

➢ China Academy of Launch Vehicle Technology 中国运载火箭技术研究院(又名中国航天科技集团有限公司第一研究院): 成立于1957年11月16日,隶属于中国航天科技集团有限公司,是中国航天事业的发祥地,是我国历史最久、规模最大的导弹武器和运载火箭研制、试验和生产基地。

➢ sci-tech empowerment 科技赋能:利用现代科学技术手段,对人类社会、生产生活、管理等各个领域进行深入改造和创新,使其更加智能化、高效化、便捷化、可持续化。

Exercises

1. Dealing with Unfamiliar Words

Fill in the blanks in the following sentences with the correct form of the words from the box.

commission	legislate	prominent	deliberate	moderate
forge	implication	deputy	deploy	delegate
consecutive	configure	devastate	manufacture	navigate

(1) Coventry City have proved untouchable this season—they've just won their sixth _____ game.

(2) Until now this _____ disease has been unpreventable.

(3) The city council's failure to take action on the _____ irratated the community.

(4) The company has evolved into a major chemical _____.

(5) The jury took five days to _____ on the case.

(6) The Government set up a _____ to investigate allegations of police violence.

(7) Satellite _____ systems have become increasingly affordable and available.

(8) UN troops were _____ to keep the peace.

(9) The housing needs of the elderly, in particular, must be a _____ policy issue in years to come.

(10) Through powerful collaboration, globally-distributed teams _____ new partnerships to expand their business.

2. Reading and Understanding

Decide whether the following statements are true (T) or false (F).

(1) In its manned space program, China has signed agreements and carried out cooperation projects with France, Germany, Italy, Russia and Belgium.

(2) According to the chief of the International Energy Agency, China today is the biggest driver of clean energy technologies.

(3) The technology of "Juncao" is an economical and environmentally friendly substitute for timber as a substrate for growing mushrooms.

(4) The contribution of scientific and technological progress to the country's economic growth has exceeded 60 percent.

(5) China has established sci-tech cooperation relations with more than 116 countries and regions.

3. Translating

Translate the paragraph into Chinese.

To turn the grand blueprint drawn at the 20th CPC National Congress into reality, young people from all walks of life need to step forward to contribute as much as they can. I hope that you will continue to carry forward the spirit of serving the country by developing aviation, be of one mind for joint endeavor to promote self-reliance and self-improvement in aviation science and technology as well as the high-quality development of aviation industry. I hope that you will strive to be good young people of the new era who have lofty ideals, dare to shoulder responsibilities, and work hard, so as to make further contributions to building China into a modern socialist country in all respects and promoting the great rejuvenation of the Chinese nation at all fronts.

4. Developing Critical Thinking

   Work in pairs and discuss the following questions.

   (1) What else do you know about China's self-reliant sci-tech progress?

   (2) How do you understand that sci-tech progress will make China better?

Further Reading

Cooperation Key to Speed up Tech Breakthroughs

Greater international cooperation is needed to explore technological frontiers such as computer-brain interface technologies and artificial intelligence, which are widely seen as key future drivers of global economic growth, officials and experts said.

Highlighting that decoupling in crucial technologies will only slow down the world economy, they called on Chinese companies to have a problem-solving mindset and to accelerate the drive for breakthroughs in core sectors.

The comments came as AI is grabbing global headlines.

US company Nvidia became the world's first chipmaker with a market capitalization of over $1 trillion on Tuesday morning amid surging demand for its AI chips. Meanwhile, Tesla CEO Elon Musk's brain-implant company Neuralink said last week that it had been given the green light for its first in-human clinical trial.

Foreign Ministry spokeswoman Mao Ning said on Thursday that China firmly opposes any actions by the United States to politicize and weaponize economic, trade and technological issues.

These comments were in response to recent media reports quoting US Treasury official Paul Rosen as saying that new rules were under consideration which would restrict the flow of US investment and know-how to Chinese companies engaged in the fields of advanced semiconductors, AI and quantum computing.

But China is clear that partnership and cooperation is the only way forward if the world is to fully harness the potential offered by the technological revolution, according to experts.

This was expressed clearly by President Xi Jinping in his congratulatory message to the 2023 Zhongguancun Forum, which ended in Beijing earlier this week. Xi said in the message that China is willing to work with countries around the world to promote technological innovation to better benefit the people of all countries.

Wu Hequan, an academician at the Chinese Academy of Engineering, said international cooperation is vital to achieving scientific breakthroughs, and China and the US are highly complementary to each other in AI.

US companies are advanced in fundamental science and underlying computer algorithms, while China has a big market and rich application scenarios, and its research and development prowess in AI is also growing, Wu said.

By 2022, China had secured the top position globally in terms of the number of patent applications for AI, according to the Ministry of Industry and Information Technology.

AI technology will usher in the next digital revolution after the internet and smartphones, experts said, with Goldman Sachs forecasting that generative AI could drive a 7 percent increase in global GDP, or almost $7 trillion, over a 10-year period.

Nick Fowler, chief academic officer at Elsevier, a Netherlands-based academic publishing company, said there is enduring strength in the China-US research relationship, despite noise about the two countries decoupling.

The Field Weighted Citation Impact — a proxy measure of research quality — of China-US co-authored publications reached almost two, which is twice the world average, and higher than the performance of either China or the US alone, according to a report by Elsevier.

While Washington is imposing increasingly tighter restrictions on technology, China's central leadership is attaching greater importance to innovation-driven development.

Beijing and Shenzhen, a metropolis in Guangdong province, announced favorable policies this week to support the development of domestically developed AI chips, which are the key to the ongoing AI boom triggered by ChatGPT, an AI chatbot developed by the US company OpenAI.

Liu Qingfeng, chairman of Chinese AI company iFlytek Co, said, "Chinese companies must devote big, real money to research and development in fundamental science to achieve breakthroughs in AI."

So far, China has developed at least 79 AI large-language models, or rivals of ChatGPT, according to the Institute of Scientific and Technical Information of China.

When it comes to computer-brain interface technology, which enables a person to control an external device using brain signals, China is also making steady progress.

A team led by Duan Feng, a professor at Nankai University in Tianjin, completed the world's first interventional brain-computer interface experiment in a nonhuman primate earlier this month.

(Source: http://english.scio.gov.cn/in-depth/2023-06/02/content_86108529.htm)

Unit 4

China's Economy

Text A

A Look at China's Economic Resilience amid Sluggish Global Growth

Despite sluggish global growth, China has navigated economic headwinds with an effective policy mix, which has facilitated an overall recovery so far this year and paved the way for sustained development in the long run.

As per experts, the Chinese economy maintained a consistent upward trajectory during the first half (H1) of this year, marked by improved structure and enhanced quality.

The gross domestic product increased 5.5 percent from a year ago in H1, quicker than the 3 percent expansion of 2022. Consumption, serving as a more forceful driving force, contributed 77.2 percent of the economic growth, and consumer prices returned to a month-on-month increase in July, indicating recovering demand.

"China's growth was significantly faster than that of the major developed economies across the world against the backdrop of an increasing risk of global recession, thereby demonstrating a great economic resilience," said Liu Xueyan, a researcher with the Chinese Academy of Macroeconomic Research.

Amidst aggravating global inflation, China has successfully ensured both price stability and economic advancement through its comprehensive industrial production system, secure energy and food supply, as well as targeted and effective policies, Liu added.

Yan Min, a research fellow with the State Information Center, pointed out that China's growth features high quality, guarantees people's well-being, and has the potential and vitality to withstand shocks and achieve long-term, sound development.

Higher Quality

China's economy made solid progress in high-quality development in the January-June period.

The service sector contributed 66.1 percent of the economic growth, higher than the secondary industry. High-tech investment climbed 12.5 percent year on year, faster than the growth rate of total investment. In a sign of improved innovation capacity, the output in the manufacturing of spacecraft equipment and lithium-ion batteries surged 22.9 percent and 29.7 percent, respectively.

The eastern regions of China continued to lead the way, while central regions strengthened their capabilities in grain production and advanced manufacturing, and the western regions continued to unlock their potential.

The Beijing-Tianjin-Hebei region, the Yangtze River Delta region, and the Guangdong-Hong Kong-Macao Greater Bay Area, which are the country's major regional drivers of growth, continued to enjoy robust growth momentum, according to Zhang Yan with a research center under the National Development and Reform Commission (NDRC).

As China is picking up pace in building a national unified market, strengthened regional coordination will expand effective investment and spur local economic powerhouses, thus promoting the economic recovery of the whole country, Zhang said.

Intensified Efforts

As the economy still faces challenges and the recovery foundation is not stable, China has stepped up measures to boost confidence, ensure sustained recovery and promote high-quality development.

Authorities have doubled down efforts to boost the development of private businesses.

A policy guideline was issued last month to address key concerns of private businesses, including market entry, fair competition, legal protection, financing support, intellectual property rights protection, and innovation input.

The policy effects have reverberated across the private economy. The development index of China's small and medium-sized enterprises rose for a second straight month in July, indicating an improvement in market expectations.

Alongside the focus on private enterprises, there has been a heightened emphasis on bolstering consumption, which plays a fundamental role in driving economic growth. Consumer spending has been encouraged on a wide range of goods and services, including new energy vehicles, home appliances, electronics, catering and tourism.

"Restoring and expanding consumption is the main focus and urgent task to promote the sustained improvement of China's economy," said Wang Changlin, vice president of the Chinese Academy of Social Sciences.

As there are still constraints on the recovery and expansion of consumption, "more measures should be adopted to raise people's incomes, boost social security benefits, improve public services and increase the supply of quality goods and services, to ensure that people can spend, dare to spend and are willing to spend," Wang said.

Benefitting from the efficacy of current policies and with additional measures in the pipeline, the Chinese economy is expected to maintain its steady trajectory during the rest of the year.

"We have the confidence, conditions and capability to ensure a better economic structure and a stronger growth momentum, sustain a sound development trend, and achieve the full-year economic and social development targets," said Li Hui, an NDRC official.

(Source: http://english.scio.gov.cn/in-depth/2023-08/15/content_102942344.htm)

Language Focus

Words and Expressions

sluggish *adj.* 缓慢的，迟缓的	moving, acting, or working with less than usual speed or energy
trajectory *n.* 轨道；(事业等的)发展轨迹，起落	a path, progression, or line of development resembling a physical curved path that an object follows after it has been thrown or shot into the air
backdrop *n.* (事件的)背景	the general situation in which particular events happen
macroeconomic *adj.* 宏观经济的	of or connected with financial systems at a national level
withstand *v.* 经受住，承受住	to be strong enough, or not be changed by something, or to oppose a person or thing successfully
robust *adj.* 稳固的，健全的	strong and unlikely to break or fail
spur *v.* 促进，加速，刺激(某事发生)	to encourage an activity or development or make it happen faster
reverberate *v.* 震撼；产生广泛影响	if an event or idea reverberates somewhere, it has an effect on everyone or everything in a place or group
bolster *v.* 加强，改善；鼓舞	to support or improve something or make it stronger

catering *n.* 饮食服务；酒席承办	relating to the activity of providing food and drink at events, for organizations, etc.
constraint *n.* 限制，束缚	something that controls what you do by keeping you within particular limits
efficacy *n.* 功效，效力	the ability, especially of a medicine or a method of achieving something, to produce the intended result
pipeline *n.* （供应货物、信息等的）渠道，途径	a plan, product, etc. that is in the pipeline is being discussed or prepared and will be produced or finished in the future

Notes and Explanations

➢ Beijing-Tianjin-Hebei region 京津冀地区：包括北京、天津两大直辖市以及河北省部分城市，是中国的"首都经济圈"。京津冀地缘相接、人缘相亲，地域一体、文化一脉，历史渊源深厚，交往半径相宜，完全能够相互融合、协同发展。京津冀位于东北亚中国地区环渤海心脏地带，是中国北方经济规模最大、最具活力的地区。

➢ Guangdong-Hong Kong-Macao Greater Bay Area 粤港澳大湾区：指广东省、香港特别行政区和澳门特别行政区在珠江三角洲地区合作建设的综合性区域，包括香港特别行政区、澳门特别行政区和广东省广州市、深圳市、珠海市、佛山市、惠州市、东莞市、中山市、江门市、肇庆市。粤港澳大湾区以香港、澳门、广州、深圳四大中心城市作为区域发展的核心引擎，目的是加快珠江三角洲地区经济、科技、人文等方面的发展，打造具有国际影响力的城市群和世界级湾区经济体。粤港澳大湾区是我国开放程度最高、经济活力最强的区域之一，在国家发展大局中具有重要战略地位。

➢ National Development and Reform Commission (NDRC) 中华人民共和国国家发展和改革委员会（简称"国家发展改革委"）：国务院的组成部门，前身是国家计划委员会、国家发展计划委员会。国家发展改革委是综合研究拟订经济和社会发展政策，进行总量平衡，指导总体经济体制改革的宏观调控部门。国家发展改革委贯彻落实党中央关于发展改革工作的方针政策和决策部署，在履行职责过程中坚持和加强党对发展改革工作的集中统一领导。

Exercises

1. Dealing with Unfamiliar Words

   Match the words in the left with their definitions.

   (1) backdrop   a path, progression, or line of development

   (2) catering   the ability to recover after something bad has happened

   (3) trajectory   the general situation in which particular events happen

   (4) resilience   the business of producing goods in large numbers

   (5) capability   the business or activity of providing food and drink at events

   (6) manufacturing   the ability or power to do something

   (7) inflation   the act of using, eating, or drinking something

   (8) consumption   an increase in prices over time, causing a reduction in the value of money

2. Reading and Understanding

   Decide whether the following statements are true (T) or false (F).

   (1) The Chinese economy continued to grow during the first half (H1) of this year.

   (2) Due to the global recession, the speed of China's economic development was outpaced by developed countries.

   (3) Central China's advanced manufacturing has caught up with that of Eastern China.

   (4) The policy guideline of China had a positive impact on its medium-sized enterprises.

   (5) It is urgent for China to take measures to boost people's consumption.

3. Questions for Discussion

   Work in small groups and discuss the following questions.

   (1) China can facilitate a domestic overall recovery against the backdrop of sluggish global growth. What do you think are the main reasons for this?

   (2) What are the benefits of building a national unified market in China?

   (3) Why boostering consumer spending is so important? What can be done to spur domestic consumption?

4. Translating

   Translate the following paragraph into English.

   ### 中国雄安——千年大计、国家大事

   随着中国进入新时代，蕴育着勃勃生机的雄安新区吸引了世界的目光。河北雄安新区地处北京、天津、保定腹地，距北京、天津均为105千米。在中国，它所在的京津冀地区极具发展潜力,京津冀协同发展战略自2014年开始全面实施,深入推进。习近平总书记指出,雄安新区将是我们留给子孙后代的历史遗产,必须坚持"世界眼光、国际标准、中国特色、高点定位"理念,努力打造贯彻新发展理念的创新发展示范区。

Text B

China Ramps up Macro Control for Stable Economic Growth

China's top leadership has convened a crucial meeting that set the economic policy agenda for the rest of the year with clear macro policy steps to navigate new situations facing the country's "tortuous recovery."

Currently, China's economy is meeting with new difficulties and challenges, which mainly arise from insufficient domestic demand, difficulties in the operation of some enterprises, risks and hidden dangers in key areas, as well as a grim and complex external environment, according to the meeting held by the Political Bureau of the Communist Party of China (CPC) Central Committee on Monday.

The world's second-largest economy secured a 5.5-percent GDP expansion in the first half (H1) of the year — quicker than 2022 and this year's first quarter, while certain indicators showed a trend of decline and fluctuations.

"We cannot perceive this round of recovery from an old perspective," said Liu Yuanchun, president of the Shanghai University of Finance and Economics. "Post-COVID recovery occurs in stages, and fluctuations in indicators and expectations are normal."

China's post-pandemic recovery is a "wave-like" and tortuous progress, with the country's long-term sound economic fundamentals remaining unchanged, the meeting noted.

Leveraging Fiscal, Monetary Tools

To combat the challenges, the central leadership emphasized the need for precise and forceful macroeconomic regulation, focusing on strengthening counter-cyclical regulation and adopting more policy options.

The meeting called for the continuation of a proactive fiscal policy and a prudent monetary policy and leveraging the role of quantitative and structural monetary tools to support the real economy, scientific and technological innovation, and the development of micro, small, and medium-sized enterprises.

The mentioning of "counter-cyclical" adjustment signaled that the monetary policy would be intensified and the policy orientation is to stabilize growth, so there might be an increase in the intensity of credit supply in the future, said a research note by China International Capital Corporation Limited after the meeting.

"The proactive fiscal policy will continue to focus on helping enterprises overcome difficulties and promoting investment, while the monetary policy will adopt price-based instruments and focus on optimizing the structural monetary policy tools," said Feng

Xuming, a Chinese Academy of Social Sciences (CASS) research fellow.

Boosting Domestic Demand

The CPC Central Committee has urged active expansion of domestic demand, particularly on bolstering consumption, and called for accelerating government investment to drive overall investment.

Consumption in key sectors such as automobiles, electronic products, and household items will be bolstered. Spending on services, including sports, leisure, culture, and tourism, is also encouraged, according to the meeting.

With a contribution of 77.2 percent to economic growth, consumption has played an increasingly prominent role in driving China's economy in H1.

China's top economic planner has mapped out measures to restore and expand consumption in a wide-ranging plan to bolster growth. Detailed plans on promoting the consumption of automobiles, electronic products, and household items have been unveiled this month.

Chen Lifen, a researcher at the Development Research Center of the State Council, stressed the need to expand domestic consumption to achieve development goals considering a lack of driving forces in global growth and a slowdown in international trade.

"With the gradual implementation of policies to expand domestic demand, investment and consumption are expected to maintain stable growth in the second half of the year, further enhancing the resilience and stability of China's economic development," said Chen.

The meeting stressed that government investment should better drive overall investment, with faster issuance and use of local government special-purpose bonds.

In H1, the country saw a slow issuance of special bonds, and there is still a quota of 1.6 trillion yuan (about 224.1 billion U.S. dollars) of bonds waiting to be issued in the second half, said Wen Bin, the chief economist at China Minsheng Bank. He expected that the issuance of special bonds would accelerate in the third quarter to support infrastructure investment and stabilize the economy.

Defusing Risks to Achieve High-Quality Growth

In pursuit of high-quality development, the CPC Central Committee stressed the importance of fostering strategic emerging industries and promoting the integration of the digital economy with advanced manufacturing and modern services.

The real estate market also received attention. The meeting called for concrete efforts to prevent and defuse risks in key areas and adjust and optimize real estate policies promptly in response to the new situation that "major changes have taken place in the relationship between supply and demand in China's real estate market."

"It is a precise judgment on the changes in the supply-demand relationship and the structure of China's real estate market under the new situation, sending a clear signal for timely adjustment and optimization of policies to promote the stable and healthy development of the real estate market," said Zou Linhua with the CASS.

Policy toolkits should be well utilized with city-specific measures to meet residents' essential housing demand and their needs for better housing, and advance the stable and sound development of the real estate market, according to the meeting.

China will likely adopt more supportive measures in the property sector in the rest of the year, which will stimulate residential purchasing and effectively alleviate risks for real estate enterprises, said Lian Ping, the chief economist at Zhixin Investment Research Institute.

Wen Bin with China Minsheng Bank pointed out that the real estate policies are still geared towards risk prevention, indicating that the goal of policy adjustments is to ease the overly strict policies in the previous stage and prevent risks from worsening.

"Real estate will not be used as a short-term means to stimulate the economy," Wen stressed.

(Source: http://english.scio.gov.cn/in-depth/2023-07/26/content_95168500.htm)

Language Focus

Words and Expressions

convene v. 召集，集合	to bring together a group of people for a meeting, or to meet for a meeting
navigate v. 成功应对（困难处境）	to lead a company, activity, etc. in a particular direction, or to deal effectively with a difficult situation
tortuous adj. 曲折的；转弯抹角的	with many turns and changes of direction; not direct or simple
grim adj. （形势）严峻的	worrying, without hope
leverage v. 充分利用（资源、观点等）	to use something that you already have in order to achieve something new or better
fiscal adj. 财政的	of or relating to the public treasury or financial matters in general

monetary *adj.* 货币的，金融的		relating to money, especially the money supply of a country
proactive *adj.* 积极主动的		intending or intended to produce a good result or avoid a problem, rather than waiting until there is a problem
prudent *adj.* 谨慎的，慎重的		showing good judgment in avoiding risks and uncertainties; careful
orientation *n.* 目标，定位		the particular interests, activities, or aims of an organization or business
pursuit *n.* 追求，寻找		the act of trying to achieve a plan, activity, or situation, usually over a long period of time
defuse *v.* 缓和，平息		to make a difficult or dangerous situation calmer by reducing or removing its cause

Notes and Explanations

➢ China International Capital Corporation Limited 中国国际金融股份有限公司（简称"中金公司"）：成立于1995年，总部位于北京。在"做中国自己的国际投行"的公司愿景下，中金公司为我国融入全球资本市场的竞争与合作作出了贡献。

➢ Chinese Academy of Social Sciences 中国社会科学院：在中国科学院哲学社会科学部的基础上于1977年建立，是中国哲学社会科学研究的最高学术机构和综合研究中心。中国社会科学院以学科齐全、人才集中、资料丰富的优势，在中国改革开放和现代化建设的进程中，进行创造性的理论探索和政策研究，肩负着从整体上提高中国人文社会科学水平的使命。

➢ China Minsheng Bank 中国民生银行：1996年在北京成立，是中国首家由民营企业发起设立的全国性股份制商业银行。作为中国银行业改革的试验田，民生银行锐意改革、积极进取，业务不断拓展，规模不断扩大，为推动中国银行业的改革创新作出了积极贡献。

Exercises

1. Dealing with Unfamiliar Words

Fill in the blanks in the following sentences with the correct form of the words from the box.

leverage	optimize	alleviate	proactive	convene
prudent	navigate	tortuous	fiscal	monetary
defuse	pursuit	supportive	precise	promptly

(1) The new systems have been _____ for running the new-version programme.

(2) Companies are going to have to be more _____ about environmental management.

(3) The path to peace seems at last to be clear, although it may be a long and _____ one.

(4) They insisted that the deal is fiscally _____ and would not put the city budget at risk.

(5) Last, but not least, it had some vague powers as far as international _____ policy was concerned.

(6) We help new home-buyers _____ the complex and often confusing process of purchasing a property.

(7) The prime minister _____ (a meeting of) his cabinet to discuss the matter.

(8) We can gain a market advantage by _____ our network of partners.

(9) The medicine did nothing to _____ her discomfort.

(10) The two groups will meet next week to try to _____ the crisis.

2. Reading and Understanding

Decide whether the following statements are true (T) or false (F).

(1) Insufficiency of domestic consumption is posing challenges to China's economy.

(2) To stabilize economic growth, China should weaken the role of monetary policy.

(3) In H1, consumption has been the most important factor in driving China's economy.

(4) Demand will exceed supply in China's real estate market following the release of policies.

(5) Real estate policy should only exert impact for a short time to drive the economic growth.

3. Translating

Translate the following paragraph into Chinese.

Chinese authorities are stepping up support for micro, small and medium-sized enterprises as well as self-employed individuals by extending and improving a series of preferential tax and fee policies amid broader efforts to drive development of the private sector. Such efforts will greatly boost the vitality and improve operating conditions of MSMEs and self-employed individuals. It will in turn drive them to offer more jobs and promote the development of the private economy.

4. Developing Critical Thinking

Work in pairs and discuss the following questions.

(1) What is "high-quality development" in your view?

(2) To achieve high-quality development in China, what can be done for different market players?

Further Reading

Globalization of Renminbi to Boost Stability

The internationalization of the renminbi (RMB) is gathering momentum, and such a trend will help facilitate China's further opening-up and encourage the country's global trade and investment, scholars and analysts said.

Their remarks came after global financial messaging platform Swift announced on Thursday that the RMB's share in global payments had increased for five consecutive months to 2.77 percent in June, the highest level since January 2022 when the share was 3.2 percent.

The RMB's share stood at 2.54 percent in May, Swift said, adding that the Chinese currency has retained its position as the fifth most active currency for global payments by value.

As of the end of 2022, the Renminbi Internationalization Index increased by 18.08 percent from the previous year and is maintaining a long-term upward trend, a research report released on Saturday by the International Monetary Institute at the Renmin University of China showed.

Speaking on Saturday at a forum held in Beijing, Chen Yulu, president of Nankai University, said the RMB is gaining momentum in its level of internationalization, and "is expected to become the most dynamic and promising global high-quality public product".

Noting that the RMB has become one of the major international currencies, Chen said that efforts are necessary on three fronts to strengthen its globalization further.

A modern industrial system that is underpinned by the real economy should be completed, he said.

"Progress is also needed in deepening financial market reforms and in the establishment of infrastructure for RMB globalization. In addition, there must be a high level of balance between the institutional opening-up of China's financial system and its risk control," he said.

Global challenges, such as the impact of the pandemic and geopolitical conflicts, have made the problem of insufficient international currency supply more urgent, Chen said.

"The internationalization of the RMB offers emerging markets and developing economies a new option, and also drives the international monetary system toward a direction of diversified competition. This will, in turn, enhance global economic stability," he said.

On Thursday, the People's Bank of China (PBOC), the nation's central bank, adjusted several rules to allow businesses to borrow more overseas, opening up the door for more foreign capital inflow.

The macro-prudential adjustment parameter — a multiplier that decides the upper limit of outstanding cross-border financing available to corporates and financial institutions — was revised from 1.25 to 1.5, effective immediately, according to the PBOC.

Wang Fang, deputy dean of the School of Finance at Renmin University of China, said that global trade and investment cooperation is a viable way for RMB internationalization.

She suggested that RMB internationalization be steadily promoted via various levels of economic and trade cooperation, such as the Regional Comprehensive Economic Partnership agreement, and that conditions for RMB transaction be promptly improved.

Eddie Yue, chief executive of the Hong Kong Monetary Authority, said that currently, businesses across the world are seeking risk diversification in a highly uncertain macroeconomic environment, which might boost demand for the renminbi.

Also, while central banks in major economies have significantly raised interest rates, China's comparatively low interest rates have bolstered the RMB's attractiveness as an international financing currency, he said.

On Friday, the central parity rate of the RMB strengthened 10 pips to 7.1456 against the dollar, according to the China Foreign Exchange Trade System.

(Source: http://english.scio.gov.cn/in-depth/2023-07/24/content_94513684.htm)

Unit 5

China's Environment

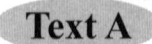

Guideline Targets Health of Yangtze

New Mechanism to Help Shore up Ecosystems in the River Basin

A plan to establish an environmental evaluation and assessment system that prioritizes the health of aquatic ecosystems in the Yangtze River will help address "weak links" in the conservation of Asia's longest watercourse and better meet people's ever-growing demands for a beautiful environment in the region, officials and experts said.

In a move to further enhance the protection of China's mother river, the Ministry of Ecology and Environment, together with the National Development and Reform Commission and the ministries of water resources and agriculture and rural affairs, issued a guideline for the trial implementation of the system in late June, vowing to conduct the first evaluations and assessments in the 17 provincial-level regions in the Yangtze basin in 2025.

In 2023 and 2024, pilot programs will be rolled out in these regions to fine-tune the evaluation and assessment mechanism before its 2025 debut and also to set benchmark indexes for the 50 water bodies that will be covered, according to the guideline.

The programs will be carried out in these water bodies, including the main stream of the Yangtze, its major tributaries and key lakes and reservoirs in the basin, while taking into account their unique characteristics.

Currently, there are 10 environmental assessment indexes for rivers, 11 for lakes and 6 for reservoirs. But these types of water bodies have three indexes in common — one that assesses the number of fish species, one for the number of key state-protected aquatic organisms and one that measures human influence on the habitats of these animals.

Rivers and lakes have two indexes in common — one that looks at the number of macrobenthic species and another focusing on the proportion of natural shorelines.

The mechanism's design will adhere to the principle of prioritizing environmental protection and letting nature restore itself, the Ministry of Ecology and Environment said in a media release after the guideline was made public.

With the health of aquatic ecosystems as the core, its index system aims to promote concerted efforts to improve the management of aquatic environments' ecosystems, as well as water resources, it said.

The indexes that will be part of the evaluation and assessment mechanism — all of which will employ well-established monitoring methods — have been chosen from almost 200 that have been applied in other mechanisms domestically and overseas, it continued.

Scores will be assigned to each water body and region. The scores for each of the water bodies will be calculated based on comparisons between the current actual index levels and the expected levels, though the weight of each index will be different.

The scores for each provincial region will be based on the sum of the scores for all the water bodies under their jurisdiction. Furthermore, the efforts that these regions have made to protect these water bodies will also be evaluated, the guideline said, adding that the degree of improvement in water quality will be a key consideration.

Based on their overall performances, the 17 provincial-level regions will each be assigned one of three grades: excellent, good or poor.

Resolving "Weak Links"

Wang Dong, deputy chief engineer of Chinese Academy of Environmental Planning, said the guideline was introduced against the backdrop that the country's efforts to conserve the Yangtze over the past 10 years have seen sweeping, historic and transformative changes, but there are still some prominent environmental and ecological problems in the basin.

In 2022, the water quality in 98.1 percent of the monitoring sections in the Yangtze basin stood at or above Grade II, up 15.8 percentage points from 2016, he said, adding that 2022 was the third consecutive year that the water quality throughout Yangtze's main stream had reached that grade level.

China has a six-tier quality system for surface water, with Grade I being the best quality and below Grade V the worst.

Wang, however, also noted severe ecological imbalances in some of the water bodies in the basin. "With frequent outbreaks of blue algae and water blooms, some water bodies have experienced remarkable declines in their biological diversities," he said.

Some areas in the basin are also still plagued by severe water pollution, which is particularly bad during flood season, and black and odorous water bodies have not yet been completely eradicated, he said.

If these "weak links" cannot be resolved, he stressed, the country will not be able to realize its vision of "Building a Beautiful China".

The environmental evaluation and assessment mechanism outlined in the guideline, which focuses on the health of aquatic ecosystems, will help shore up these weak spots in a more targeted manner, Wang said.

He also noted that the introduction of the mechanism would serve as a measure to implement the Yangtze River Protection Law, which states that the state must adopt a targeted accountability and performance evaluation system for environmental protection work in the Yangtze basin.

As the country's first legislation on a specific river basin, the law took effect on March 1, 2021.

The guideline has sent a clear signal that the country will make full use of performance evaluation as a means to guide local governments to ramp up water conservation and beef up ecological remediation efforts.

For the People

The document stressed that the results of evaluations and assessments should be in line with people's expectations, he said. It also underscored the importance of increasing people's sense of happiness and security by meeting their water consumption demands and passion for water-related recreational activities.

Huo Chuanlin, head of the Ministry of Ecology and Environment's administration for the Taihu Lake basin and the East China Sea, also highlighted the people-centered philosophy in the guideline.

With a focus on aquatic organisms rather than physical and chemical data as the key factor, the environmental evaluation and assessment mechanism in the document is more people-friendly, he said.

As important indicators of the condition of the waters they live in, he said, these organisms can give the public an intuitive feeling about ecological and environmental improvements.

Xu Chong, head of the Ministry of Ecology and Environment's bureau that oversees the Yangtze, said that under the evaluation and assessment mechanism, index levels will be set in accordance with the conditions in the various water bodies.

The guideline stipulates that the differences in environmental and ecological conditions and economic development levels, as well as the characteristics of different types of water bodies, should be fully considered when setting the expected levels for the indexes, he said.

Historical records and the restoration potential of the water bodies are both key considerations that will factor in determining the expected levels, and will help guide local governments to devote more efforts to nature conservation and ecological remediation, he said.

A Welcome Change

Liu Guocai, head of the Nanjing Institute of Environmental Sciences, lauded the great importance that the guideline has attached to the aquatic ecosystems and habitats, which he emphasized were the crux of environmental and ecological problems in the Yangtze.

Despite marked improvement in its aquatic environment, the river is generally lacking fish due largely in part to damage wrought on their habitat.

He also noted the imbalance of the aquatic ecosystems that have seen declines in populations of some key fish and zooplankton species as fundamental reasons for the frequent outbreaks of blue algae and water blooms in key lakes in the Yangtze basin, including the Taihu and Dianchi lakes.

Among the indexes in the evaluation and assessment mechanism, six concern the health of aquatic ecosystems and four focus on the conservation of aquatic habitats, he stated.

The four indexes for aquatic habitat protection, for instance, aim to direct local governments to remediate damaged shorelines, restore basic ecological functions of water bodies and enhance their interconnectivity, and gradually eliminate improper human activities in aquatic habitats, he said.

Regarding the restoration of the aquatic organism population, the guideline stressed the principle of letting nature restore itself.

"This will help local governments avoid pursuing short-term results by overusing artificial means for conservation and remediation, which may negatively affect the health of aquatic ecosystems," he said.

He stressed the evaluation and assessment mechanism is not meant to depopulate the area.

Rather, it aims to push local governments to better implement the ecological civilization philosophy of respecting, accommodating and protecting nature, to explore a development path that features harmonious coexistence between humanity and nature, and to better balance and coordinate economic development and environmental protection, he said.

As part of its efforts to promote ecological stability, the nation began a 10-year fishing moratorium on key areas in all natural waterways of the Yangtze River, including its major tributaries and lakes, on January 1, 2021.

A full fishing ban was first implemented in 332 conservation areas in the Yangtze basin in January 2020, and the ban has since been expanded.

According to the Ministry of Agriculture and Rural Affairs, in these conservation areas alone, more than 84,000 fishing boats have been decommissioned, and 180,000 people have left the fishing industry.

With no available experiences from home and abroad to draw on, the evaluation and assessment work in the Yangtze basin is meant to break new ground, and a lot of effort will be needed to establish it properly, Liu stressed.

The vast stretches of the basin and the great variations of the conditions in the areas in it mean that the index system for the evaluation and assessment mechanism "will have to be consistently improved," he said.

(Source: https://www.chinadaily.com.cn/a/202308/16/WS64dc141aa31035260b81c5d8.html)

Language Focus

Words and Expressions

aquatic *adj.* 水生的；水中的；水栖的	living or growing in water
ecosystem *n.* 生态系统	all the animals and plants in a particular area, and the way in which they are related to each other and to their environment
vow *v.* 发誓；立誓；起誓	to make a serious promise to yourself or someone else
mechanism *n.* 机制，构造	a system or a way of behaving that helps a living thing to avoid or protect itself from something difficult or dangerous
benchmark *n.* 基准	something that is used as a standard by which other things can be judged or measured
tributary *n.* 支流	a steam or river that flows into a larger river
reservoir *n.* 水库；蓄水池	a lake, especially an artificial one, where water is stored before it is supplied to people's houses
jurisdiction *n.* 管辖权；管辖范围；管辖区域；司法权	the right to use an official power to make legal decisions, or the area where this right exists
ecological *adj.* 生态的	connected with the way plants, animals, and people are related to each other and to their environment

algae *n.* 藻类；海藻	a very simple plant without stems or leaves that grows in or near water
eradicate *v.* 根除；消灭；杜绝	to completely get rid of something such as a disease or a social problem
intuitive *adj.* 直觉的	an intuitive idea is based on a feeling rather than on knowledge or facts
stipulate *v.* 规定；明确要求	if an agreement, law, or rule stipulates something, it must be done
laud *v.* 称赞；赞扬	to praise someone or something

Notes and Explanations

➢ Yangtze River 长江：属太平洋水系，全长6363千米，是中国第一大河。长江干流自西而东横贯中国中部，流经中国青藏高原、横断山区、云贵高原、四川盆地和长江中下游平原。长江是中华民族的母亲河之一，长江流域是中华民族的重要发祥地。

➢ Building a Beautiful China 建设美丽中国："美丽中国"是中国共产党第十八次全国代表大会提出的概念，强调把生态文明建设放在突出地位，融入经济建设、政治建设、文化建设、社会建设各方面和全过程。

➢ The Yangtze River Protection Law《中华人民共和国长江保护法》：为了加强长江流域生态环境保护和修复，促进资源合理高效利用，保障生态安全，实现人与自然和谐共生、中华民族永续发展制定的法律。2020年12月26日，中华人民共和国第十三届全国人民代表大会常务委员会第二十四次会议通过该法，自2021年3月1日起施行。

Exercises

1. Dealing with Unfamiliar Words

   Match the words in the left with their definitions.

   (1) tributary   to completely get rid of something such as a disease or a social problem

   (2) consecutive   the right to use an official power to make legal decisions

   (3) eradicate   to praise someone or something

   (4) reservoir   a lake, where water is stored before it is supplied to people's houses

   (5) jurisdiction a stream or river that flows into a larger river

(6) algae   a system or a way of behaving that helps a living thing to avoid or protect itself from something difficult or dangerous

(7) laud   a very simple plant without stems or leaves that grows in or near water

(8) mechanism   numbers or periods of time follow one after another without an interruption

2. Reading and Understanding

Decide whether the following statements are true (T) or false (F).

(1) China has a six-tier quality system for surface water, with Grade V being the best quality and below Grade I the worst.

(2) Rivers and lakes have two indexes in common — one that looks at the number of macrobenthic species and another focusing on the proportion of natural shorelines.

(3) The pilot programs will be carried out in these water bodies, including the main stream of the Yangtze, its major tributaries and key lakes and reservoirs in the basin, without taking into account their unique characteristics.

(4) Under the evaluation and assessment mechanism, index levels will be set in accordance with the conditions in the various water bodies.

(5) As part of its efforts to promote ecological stability, China began a 10-year fishing moratorium on key areas in all natural waterways of the Yangtze River, including its major tributaries and lakes, on March 1, 2021.

3. Questions for Discussion

Work in small groups and discuss the following questions.

(1) How can the new mechanism help shore up ecosystems in the river basin?

(2) Why should the environmental evaluation and assessment system be in line with people's expectations?

(3) Regarding the restoration of the aquatic organism population, what is the meaning of letting nature restore itself in the guideline?

4. Translating

Translate the following paragraph into English.

    要像保护眼睛一样保护生态环境，像对待生命一样对待生态环境。多谋打基础、利长远的善事，多干保护自然、修复生态的实事，多做治山理水、显山露水的好事，让群众望得见山、看得见水、记得住乡愁，让自然生态美景永驻人间，还自然以宁静、和谐、美丽。

Text B

Green Lifestyle Gains Traction Among China's Gen Z

Having been discarded in the dust in a corner of a small alley, a little potted succulent plant caught the eye of Zhu Xuan, who was scouring the streets in Shanghai with her friends for "treasures" last summer.

"It was still full of life. It was a pity that someone had thrown it away," says Zhu. "So I picked it up and now it's on my desk. I feel refreshed whenever I see it."

A 20-year-old college student, Zhu is a fan of "stooping," a campaign that encourages people to pick up unwanted items on the street for reuse. It first became trendy in New York in 2019 and is now drawing attention in China as young people grow more alarmed at the waste of resources.

Zhu is one of the many young Chinese who are increasingly aware of the environmental impact of their ways of living and who are trying to leave their green footprints on the country's path toward more sustainable development.

China marks its first National Ecology Day on Tuesday amid efforts to enhance public awareness and actions to protect the ecological environment. Gen Zers are making a difference in various ways, including stooping, joining online low-carbon initiatives, or choosing green packaging for commodities.

A table, a chair, a mattress, a toilet bowl and even a bathtub — Zhu was impressed by the variety of discarded items she encountered on the narrow streets and alleys during her stooping quests.

"These experiences have made me realize how our daily behaviors matter to the environment, and how important it is to recycle resources and avoid waste," she says.

Joining stooping activities also generates new friends for Zhu, who admitted that she would have felt awkward if doing it alone.

"We never felt like we were picking up trash. Everybody was trying to find something still valuable, like treasure hunting. It was really fun," said Zhu.

Stooping appeals to young people as a way of building social bonds among people with a similar interest in environment protection, according to Nan Zheng, the founder of online stooping accounts for more than a dozen cities, including Shanghai, Qingdao, Hangzhou and Xi'an.

Apart from connecting people for offline stooping activities, these accounts also share online information about unwanted items that may be wanted or needed by others. They have attracted the engagement of over 50,000 users, both online and offline, since November 2022, when Nan started his first stooping account.

Young people are the mainstay of used goods transactions in China, with those aged between 25 and 35 accounting for 45.1 percent and those aged 24 or below making up 22.6 percent, according to a research report released last November by QuestMobile, a mobile internet business intelligence services provider.

Zhuanzhuan, a major online platform for second-hand goods transactions in China, calculated that 668,000 tonnes of carbon emissions were prevented through the circulation of used items on the platform last year, equivalent to the emissions produced by a petrol-driven car traveling 90,000 times around the equator.

Having grown up in the internet era, Gen Zers naturally leverage the power of the internet in their pursuit of green living, by exploring new and innovative environmental activities.

An internet-based greening campaign, Ant Forest allows people to adopt trees by paying due contributions online or by garnering enough credits through performing low-carbon activities like taking public transportation, in exchange for a real tree nurtured in their names.

"It often introduces new species of trees, which is very novel and attractive to young people like me, and I would like to collect them all," says 24-year-old Dai Yipeng, who has been an Ant Forest user for over six years.

To earn more green credits, Dai now takes public transportation more often than before.

"Although public transport takes longer, when I realize I've actually helped plant a tree in the desert, the sense of accomplishment is unparalleled," she says.

By the end of 2022, a total of over 650 million users had joined the Ant Forest program to plant more than 400 million trees.

For 22-year-old Zhang Ruilin, a lover of sportswear, the packaging of a pair of sneakers matters almost as much as the shoes.

"Some stores use several layers of thick packaging materials for the shoes, which is a nuisance to consumers because it's heavy and troublesome to unwrap, and also environmentally unfriendly. I don't feel good when I have to throw the packaging away," says Zhang, who now prefers a brand that uses simple bags made of recycled materials.

Buying things with streamlined packaging, along with green transport, less use of plastics, saving water and electricity and reduced food waste, are among the most popular low-carbon practices in the daily lives of young Chinese, according to a report released by Alibaba and WIETOP Research earlier this year.

Compared with two to three years ago, the behaviour of young people has seen a marked increase in practices such as avoiding disposable cutlery when ordering food deliveries, and buying new-energy home appliances and eco-friendly products, the report says.

While two in three young people in China believe carbon reduction is closely related to their lives, they have concerns, too, about the quality control of low-carbon products and the lack of authoritative qualification for such products, according to the report.

The government aims to significantly increase the market share of green and low-carbon products by 2025. By 2030, these products should become the mainstay on the market, according to a plan released by several government departments, including the country's top economic planner, last year.

The future of China's green development depends much on Gen Zers like Zhu, who feels bonded by this shared interest and mission.

"I really enjoy meeting new people and doing a little something for the planet together," she says. "When more and more people come together to work for the environment, our home will become a little bit better."

(Source: http://english.scio.gov.cn/chinavoices/2023-08/16/content_103402380.htm)

Language Focus

Words and Expressions

succulent　*adj.*　多汁的		juicy and good to eat
scour　*v.*　冲刷；擦净		to clean something very thoroughly by rubbing it with a rough material
trendy　*adj.*　时髦的		influenced by the most fashionable styles and ideas
mattress　*n.*　床垫		the soft part of a bed that you lie on
mainstay　*n.*　支柱		the most important part of something, that makes it possible for it to be successful or to continue to exist
garner　*v.*　获得；收集		to take or collect something, especially information or support

nurture *v.* 培养；养护	to feed and take care of a child or a plant while it is growing
streamline *v.* 使效率更高	to make something such as a business, organization, etc. work more simply and effectively
cutlery *n.* 餐具（刀、叉和匙）	knives, forks, and spoons that you use for eating and serving food
authoritative *adj.* 权威的	someone or something that is authoritative has a lot of knowledge of a particular subject

Notes and Explanations

➢ stooping：本义是弯腰，引申为捡拾还有使用价值的垃圾，即把废弃物品捡回来，进行旧物回收与改造、循环利用的生活方式，参与stooping的人称为"旧物猎人"。

➢ Ant Forest 蚂蚁森林：一项旨在带动公众低碳减排的公益项目，每个人的低碳行为在蚂蚁森林里可计为"绿色能量"。"绿色能量"积累到一定程度，就可以用手机申请在生态亟须修复的地区种下一棵真树，或者在生物多样性亟须保护的地区"认领"保护权益。

➢ QuestMobile 北京贵士信息科技有限公司：中国专业的移动互联网商业智能服务商。该公司旗下拥有多条数据服务产品线，服务内容覆盖数据统计、数据分析、数据挖掘等，可以为企业提供完整的移动大数据解决方案，完善企业内部数据运营，绘制移动产品生命周期全貌，建立移动用户全视角画像，推演行业竞品行进轨迹。

Exercises

1. Dealing with Unfamiliar Words

Fill in the blanks in the following sentences with the correct form of the words from the box.

quest	authoritative	refinement	scour	cutlery
indispensable	succulent	etiquette	mainstay	streamline
moist	brew	trendy	garner	nurture

(1) The modern conservatory is not an environment for _____ plants.

(2) Milk products typical of nomadic pastoralists formed the _____ of their diet.

(3) She loves her life and is immersed in the _____ for knowledge's sake.

(4) The party _____ 70 percent of the vote.

(5) It's promoted by the natural-born hucksters within Apple because it has all the earmarks of something _____ and fashionable.

(6) The company announced it was to _____ its operations and close down three factories in the UK.

(7) The results provide the most _____ and conclusive evidence to date of some enduring inequities in participation in such facilities.

(8) I _____ the pots and pans.

(9) She observed that I was the typical American the third variant of eaters — who uses _____ in what she called the most time-consuming manner.

(10) The chicken was golden and crispy on the outside and juicy and _____ inside.

2. Reading and Understanding

Decide whether the following statements are true (T) or false (F).

(1) Joining stooping activities have made us realize how our daily behaviors matter to the environment, and how important it is to recycle resources and avoid waste, and generate new friends.

(2) Ant Forest allows people to adopt trees in exchange for a real tree cultivated in their name by paying their dues online or earning enough points through low-carbon activities such as public transportation.

(3) Stooping activity first became trendy in China in 2019.

(4) Young people are the mainstay of used goods transactions in China.

(5) In the daily lives of young people in China, purchasing things that are streamlined packaging, green transportation, reduced plastic usage, water and electricity conservation, and reduced food waste are the most popular low-carbon practices.

3. Translating

Translate the following paragraph into Chinese.

We have acted on the idea that lucid waters and lush mountains are invaluable assets. We have persisted with a holistic and systematic approach to conserving and improving mountain, water, forest, farmland, grassland, and desert ecosystems, and we have ensured stronger ecological conservation and environmental protection across the board, in all regions, and at all times. China's ecological conservation systems have been improved, the critical battle against pollution has been advanced, and solid progress has been made in promoting green, circular, and low-carbon development. This has led to historic, transformative, and comprehensive changes in ecological and environmental protection and has brought us bluer skies, greener mountains, and cleaner waters.

4. Developing Critical Thinking

   Work in pairs and discuss the following questions.

   (1) Ecological environment itself is the economy. All the ecological protection efforts will be rewarded. How do you interpret this sentence?

   (2) Why does the future of China's green development depend much on Gen Zers?

Further Reading

Eco Forum Global Highlights China's Contribution to Harmony Between Man, Nature

During the two-day-long Eco Forum Global Guiyang 2023, which concluded Sunday at the capital of southwest China's Guizhou Province, participants spoke highly of China's contribution to the global cause of promoting ecological conservation and green development.

"We are facing a global climate emergency amid a time when countries are still addressing and rebounding from the socio-economic repercussions of the COVID-19 pandemic," James George, deputy resident representative of the United Nations Development Programme in China, told Xinhua in an interview.

More efforts must be made to maintain the harmony between humanity and nature to realize the United Nations Sustainable Development Goals for a better future for both people and the planet, he added.

Talking about China's efforts in ecological conservation, he noted that "China's efforts in utilizing spatial planning to safeguard and protect key ecological function zones and fragile areas have helped improve the living environment for communities and promote biodiversity conservation."

"This is one of the lessons that could be shared with other countries in the world for strengthening conservation efforts," he noted.

During the event, Tamas Hajba, senior advisor for China and head of the Organization for Economic Co-operation and Development (OECD) Beijing Office, told Xinhua that China's role in tackling climate change and low-carbon transition is very important.

China has a lot of experiences and a lot to share with the world. It is a leading country in terms of the application of renewable energy in the world, Hajba noted.

"More importantly, China has managed to bring down the prices of renewable energies, in other words, to commercialize renewable energies much faster and much earlier than other countries," he added.

In 2022, China's renewable energy generation was equivalent to a reduction of 2.26 billion tonnes of domestic carbon dioxide emissions. Its wind power and photovoltaic product exports helped other countries reduce emissions by approximately 573 million tonnes.

The two figures added up to 2.83 billion tonnes of emissions, or about 41 percent of the world's total carbon emissions reduction converted from renewable energy, data from the National Energy Administration showed.

A firm practitioner for ecological conservation and a pilot in green development, China has also actively shared experiences and cooperated with countries globally to facilitate the harmonious coexistence of man and nature.

Pakistan's Karot hydropower project epitomizes China's global cooperation in promoting sustainable development.

The station, constructed by the China Three Gorges Corporation, can generate electricity to meet the daily power demand of about 5 million people while saving around 1.4 million tonnes of standard coal each year.

In an interview with Xinhua, Mostak Ahamed Galib, executive director of the cross-cultural communication and Belt and Road Initiative research center at the Wuhan University of Technology, hailed the China-built Padma multipurpose bridge in Bangladesh.

"Affected by rising sea level and tropical cyclones, which are heavily linked with global climate change, people's livelihoods in some parts of southwestern Bangladesh significantly deteriorated due to problems including land salinization," he said.

"The bridge has brought opportunities and new hope to people living in these areas by greatly shortening the trip to the country's capital city," he noted. With convenient transportation, thousands of domestic and foreign tourists have come to see coastal mangrove tigers in local forests.

This boosted tourism, increased the income of local residents and raised the awareness of biodiversity conservation, making people better understand how to live harmoniously with nature, he commended.

China is playing a critical role globally in terms of green development and green technology, Yanga Viwe Socikwa, a national community member of the Young Communist League of South Africa, said in an interview at the forum.

He hoped to apply China's strategies and tactics in the context of his own country and advance projects that balance environmental protection and economic growth, such as the transformation of coal mines.

Tu Ruihe, head of the UN Environment Programme China Office, expected China to continue to support international multilateral cooperation and lead global environmental governance with more active and pragmatic actions to build a community with a shared future for mankind.

"We hope that China will share experiences in the fields of low-carbon transformation, green development, environmental protection, and ecological restoration, and support developing countries in green transformation," he said in a keynote speech at the forum.

(Source: http://english.scio.gov.cn/in-depth/2023-07/11/content_91899573.htm)

Unit 6

China's Architecture

Text A

Traditional Chinese Earthen Buildings Inspire Modern Society

Carrying the genes and spirit of a nation, cultural relics and heritages are irreplaceable resources for a thriving civilization. A huge number of Chinese relics have become more popular over the past 10 years and allowed people from around the world to get to know Chinese culture better. The *Global Times* will feature a number of these "star" artifacts in this series, to make cultural relics stored in museums, heritages displayed throughout the vast land and texts written in ancient books come alive.

As Chinese President Xi Jinping has said, Chinese civilization, together with the colorful civilizations of other countries, should provide mankind with proper spiritual guidance and a strong spiritual impetus.

Today we examine the Fujian Tulou (lit: Fujian earthen buildings), a property of 46 buildings that was inscribed by UNESCO in 2008 as a World Heritage Site, to explore how it has been integrated into modern society.

In period films and TV dramas, traditional buildings are necessary to immerse audiences into the story, but these buildings and architectural designs from different dynasties or regions are more than just background settings, they are also cultural treasures that have been finding new life in modern society due to their appearances on screen.

Tulou, a traditional Chinese dwelling unique to the Hakka people living in the mountainous areas in East China's Fujian Province and South China's Guangdong Province, is one representative of traditional architecture that has been benefiting from movies and TV dramas.

The Chinese 2016 animated epic fantasy film *Big Fish & Begonia* and *Mulan*, a US fantasy action film produced by Disney in 2020, are two movies that feature tulou as a main settings. Talking about the reasoning behind his decision, director of *Big Fish & Begonia*

Liang Xuan said that they took a fancy to tulou's sense of mystery and how it invoked the feel of simple rural life.

Since the films hit the big screen, more tourists have been heading to the Fujian Tulou sites to see their beauty for themselves. One scenic spot in Fujian called Yunshuiyao was welcoming more than 4 million tourists annually before the pandemic.

These traditional buildings have also caught the attention of artists, many of whom have been lending a hand to promote these ancient dwellings and help integrate them into modern society.

Fan Yu, an urban architect, told the *Global Times* that tulou's "raw earth" touch represents a sincerity that has inspired modern architects such as Wang Shu, the designer of the Hangzhou branch of China's National Archives of Publications and Culture, to use local materials in their buildings in keeping with the Asian ethos of respecting nature and traditional culture.

Shining on the Screen

Tulou, or earthen building, is a traditional communal residence of the Hakka people, a sub-group of the Han ethnic group. Occupied by clan groups, tulou are usually large circular castle-like buildings that surround a central shrine.

The tulou of Fujian is known for its unique shape, large size and ingenious design. There are more than 20,000 tulou in southern Fujian. Looking like a large cluster of blooming flowers when seen from above, tulou easily grabs the attention of viewers when they appear on screen.

Although Disney's use of tulou in the live action *Mulan* adaptation as the main character's home was far from historically accurate, the charm of the buildings seen in the film was undeniable. Like in the film, almost everyone who resides in the same tulou are from the same clan. Living day to day in these huge buildings, residents can see neighbors and elderly folk they have known their whole lives.

These scenes reflecting traditional Chinese family culture warmed the hearts of many moviegoers.

Other traditional architecture, including grand courtyards in North China's Shanxi Province, Beijing courtyards, dwellings in the lower reaches of the Yangtze River and stilt buildings in western Sichuan Province have become more familiar to audiences through appearances in films such as the US animated *Kung Fu Panda* franchise.

Ancient Wisdom

"Tulou inspires modern architecture because it exemplifies the idea of 'people's architecture,' strengthening relationships between people," Guo Long, an architect and expert on the modernization of ancient Chinese building designs, told the *Global Times*.

Tulou is the inspiration for China's leading architecture firm Urbanus's Six Floors project, a 220-apartment collective housing complex for low income families in Guangzhou, Guangdong Province. Inheriting tulou's round multistory design, the new urban "tulou" has facilities such as a basketball court, shops and community library to better cater to people's modern lives.

"Traditional tulou inspires today's designers to think about how to enhance a sense of community through architecture. It is exactly what we miss out on in high-speed city life," Guo noted.

Lin Rigeng — the owner of China's most "artistic" tulou, the Zhencheng building in Yongding county, Fujian Province — told the *Global Times* that Chinese philosophical beauty is hidden the tulou's design.

First built more than 100 years ago, the Zhencheng tulou's configuration is based around bagua, a set of eight symbols used in Taoist cosmology to understand the world and one of the principal tools in fengshui.

"Some online reports say our tulou was built using materials such as sticky rice. This is not true. It was build using ordinary dirt, which shows the earnest and hardworking personality of we the Hakka people," Lin noted.

(Source: https://www.globaltimes.cn/page/202208/1273882.shtml)

Language Focus

Words and Expressions

relic *n.* 遗物；遗迹	an object, tradition, or system from the past that continues to exist
artifact *n.* （尤指具有史学价值的） 人工制品，制造物，手工艺品	an object that is made by a person, such as a tool or a decoration, especially one that is of historical interest
inscribe *v.* 题写；刻，雕	to write words in a book or carve them on an object
immerse *v.* 使浸没于	to put somebody or something into a liquid so that it is completely covered

dwelling *n.* 房屋，住所，住处	a house or place to live in
animate *adj.* 有生命的，活的	having life
epic *n.* （通常指描写历史题材的）长篇叙事性电影（或书籍）；史诗	a film, poem, or book that is long and contains a lot of action, usually dealing with a historical subject
invoke *v.* 援引，借助（法律）	to use a law in order to achieve something, or to mention something in order to explain something or to support your opinion or action
ethos *n.* （个人或团体的）精神特质，价值观，信条	the set of beliefs, ideas, etc. about the social behavior and relationships of a person or group
communal *adj.* 公共的；共有的；集体的；公用的	belonging to or used by a group of people rather than one single person
clan *n.* 宗族，氏族	a group of families, who originally came from the same family and have the same name
shrine *n.* 圣地；神龛；圣坛；神殿	a place for worship that is holy because of a connection with a holy person or object
ingenious *adj.* （人）灵巧的；（物品等）制作精巧的；（方法等）巧妙的	(of a person) very intelligent and skillful, or (of a thing) skillfully made or planned and involving new ideas and methods

Notes and Explanations

> *Big Fish & Begonia*《大鱼海棠》: 2016年在中国上映的动画电影。讲述了掌管海棠花生长的少女"椿"为报恩而努力复活人类男孩"鲲"的灵魂，并在本是天神的少年"湫"的帮助下与彼此纠缠的命运斗争的故事。影片取材于《庄子·逍遥游》《山海经》《搜神记》等古书，融合了"女娲补天"等中国上古神话元素，凭借出色的影片表现力斩获第15届布达佩斯国际动画电影节最佳动画长片奖。

> *Mulan*《花木兰》: 华特·迪士尼影片公司出品的真人版剧情电影，于2020年9月11日

在中国上映。该片改编自中国民间乐府诗《木兰辞》,讲述了花木兰代父从军,抵御匈奴入侵的故事。

➢ China's National Archives of Publications and Culture 中国国家版本馆(国家版本数据中心):主要承担国家版本资源规划协调、典藏展示、研究交流和出版信息服务等职责,是中华版本典藏中心、展示中心、研究中心、交流中心和国家出版信息服务中心,担负赓续中华文脉、坚定文化自信、展示大国形象、推动文明对话的重要使命。

Exercises

1. Dealing with Unfamiliar Words
   Match the words in the left with their definitions.

   (1) cosmology   the particular arrangement or pattern of a group of related things

   (2) stilt   features that were created in the past and still have historical importance

   (3) cluster   honesty

   (4) franchise   a right to sell a company's products using the company's name

   (5) configuration   the study of the nature and origin of the universe

   (6) heritage   one of a set of long pieces of wood or metal used to support a building

   (7) sincerity   a group of similar things that are close together

   (8) ingenious   (of a person) clever, original and incentive

2. Reading and Understanding
   Decide whether the following statements are true (T) or false (F).

   (1) Tulou is a representative of Chinese traditional architecture. It embodies aesthetic and cultural value.

   (2) The adaptation of tulou in films as a background setting is just because of its unique appearance.

   (3) One of the purposes of using local materials in architecture is to demonstrate a sincere respect to nature and particular culture.

   (4) The traditional tulou brings up a sense of community, providing philosophical inspiration for the new one.

   (5) Tulou in modern society is built nationwide as a charity project to provide a residence for the low-income family.

3. Questions for Discussion

Work in small groups and discuss the following questions.

(1) In which way do you think tulou can cultivates a sense of community?

(2) In your opinion, what is the meaning of tulou in modern society?

(3) Urbanus's Six Floors project is a charity project in Guangzhou and inspired by tulou. Do you think such project should be encouraged nationwide? Why or why not?

4. Translating

Translate the following paragraph into English.

受道家思想影响，古人很注重师法自然、天人合一的境界，而院落空间作为传统民居建筑的核心，是一个虚实相生的复合空间，它吸引着人们在这个围合又露天的良好空间里宴客、祭祀、婚庆、游戏、乘凉……因此，在传统民居院落空间层次布置时，古人往往会巧妙地设计人与自然的对话，在四面围合、顶部敞开的院落空间内引入假山、水体、花、草、树等；同时模仿自然风光设计非对称的自由空间层次，利用光线的明与暗、空间的曲与折、尺度的大与小、氛围的严肃与活泼、距离的离与合，在院落中营造道家自由浪漫的气氛。

Text B

Reviving Ancient Architecture

After completing its renovations, the ancient mandala-like compound Jebumgang in southwest China's Tibet Autonomous Region has drawn much public attention as a cultural and art center.

Once upon a time, a clear and melodious bell could be heard ringing from Jebumgang Lhakhang through ancient Lhasa. Today, this ancient temple, after completing its renovation, has taken on a new look as a cultural and art center.

The Past

Crisscrossed alleys paved with limestone slates and bustling open markets are what make the old town of Lhasa what it is. Following tourist maps hung across the Barkhor District, tourists can easily find a variety of old buildings and small temples. Jebumgang Lhakhang was one of them.

Located at the intersection of Ramoche Temple Road and Beijing East Road, the temple was adjacent to a fast-food restaurant and a wholesale market. Colors on the upper edge of the building had faded away over time. It was listed as a cultural relic in August 2010 during the third National Cultural Relics Census.

According to Dawa, author of *A Study of Historical Place Names in the Ancient City of Lhasa*, the place Jebumgang was named after the stupa built by the seventh Dalai Lama in the 18th century and enshrined with 100,000 statues of Master Tsongkhapa. The bottom floor of the five-storey stupa was a main hall, and people could overlook the ancient city from the top storey.

The stupa collapsed in the 19th century, and a new three-storey temple was built later on the site to make offerings to a huge clay figure of the Buddha, with 100,000 Tsongkhapa statues around it.

During the 1970s, it served as the warehouse of a local grain bureau. After the launching of China's reform and opening-up, it gradually became a trading market for *zanba*, or roasted qingke barley flour.

Renovation and Protection

Today, Jebumgang Lhakhang has taken on a brand-new look. Since 2018, the local cultural and tourism department has invested funds and organized manpower to carry out comprehensive renovations to the ancient architecture.

The roofs and floors have been reinforced with traditional supports to prevent leaking;

the columns that were in disrepair inside the buildings have been replaced; and the murals on the walls have been professionally cleaned. A variety of means were used to bring this ancient building back to life. Later, the local government entrusted a Tibetan culture and art team to transform the ancient architecture into an art center.

The team extensively looked into domestic first-class cultural venues and cases on the protection and renovation of ancient buildings. It worked with a leading domestic architectural firm for the upgrading of Jebumgang Lhakhang. Xia Yujun, executive architect responsible for the project, took the job because of his long-standing love for ancient architecture in Tibet and the entire Himalayan region.

The team carrying out the protection and renovation work overcame many difficulties. It took the team a lot of effort to just renovate the floor in order to "restore the old to make it look like the old." The floor should not only maintain its original charm, but also support the power system of the contemporary art center.

After repeated discussions, the team worked out a plan for renovating the floor. A keel was erected on the original floor, leaving enough space for pipelines. By adjusting the height of each section of the keel, the finished surface of the wooden floor was kept basically level. This not only solved the problem of unevenness of the original floor, but also alleviates the needs of hiding various fixtures, such as a pipeline.

After the plan was finalized, Xia led the workers in measuring each inch of the floor, and customized the height of the keel to ensure overall evenness of the floor. In addition to this, the team searched for suitable old wooden floors across the country, transported them to Lhasa, and then had carpenters polish, cut and assemble them according to their texture, and finally laid them on the wooden keel. To this end, Xia and his team worked on the site for more than three months in a row, making the 580-square-meter indoor space flat and uniform.

Restoration of the floor was just one hurdle the team had overcome. The temple was located in a downtown area, surrounded by residential compounds and stores. If it was to become a public cultural space, facilities, such as video surveillance, running water, and fire protection equipment, must be installed properly.

To help people understand the renovation, Xia and his team visited the surrounding residents and peddlers and explained to them why the renovation should be done.

Xia turned the stories about these transformations into short videos and shared them online, attracting tens of thousands of viewers.

Good as New

The objective of all the dedicated hard work was to bring this place full of memories back to life. Jebumgang Art Center, the first cultural and art space transformed from a protected ancient building in Tibet, was officially unveiled on July 25, 2021.

The venue's opening exhibition *Growing Ancient City* was also open to the public for free. In line with the venue's architectural characteristics, the exhibition set three chapters in the outer corridor, inner hall, and main hall of the original building.

In the outer corridor, the curatorial team used extant murals from the Qing Dynasty (1644−1911) as the theme, and fleshed it out with a large number of information found in documents, and from experts and scholars, to offer a peek into the history of the ancient city and distinctive Tibetan culture.

The inner hall displayed a series of objects related to the ancient buildings, including wooden pillars and beams that once supported the inner hall, and stone carvings excavated during the restoration process. The exhibits helped viewers find out the ingenuity in the construction of ancient buildings and the reason behind the local government and enterprises' determination to invest a lot of manpower and material resources in repairing them.

Inside the original main hall, the exhibition used a beam of light to pay tribute to the creators of Tibetan classical architecture and traditional Tibetan culture. The curatorial team also placed two sets of audio equipment for playing Tibetan classical music, which created an apt environment for audiences to experience the charm of Tibetan classical architecture in an immersive manner.

The opening exhibition lasted till the end of September in 2021. The exhibition in the outer corridor has been retained as a permanent exhibition. In the future, the art center will cooperate with top cultural and art institutions to launch public cultural education activities to spread traditional culture in contemporary languages and multiple forms.

From Jebumgang Lhakhang to Jebumgang Art Center, countless numbers of people have been dedicated to the revival of the ancient buildings. This ancient compound that was built according to a mandala structure is now showing new vitality, taking people on a journey to distinctive Tibetan culture.

(Source: http://www.chinadaily.com.cn/a/201803/21/WS5ab1ecf5a3106e7dcc144231_4.html)

Language Focus

Words and Expressions

melodious *adj.*   very pleasant to listen to
旋律优美的，悦耳的

slate *n.* 板岩；石板	a type of dark grey stone that splits easily into thin flat layers
bustling *adj.* 熙熙攘攘的；热闹的	if a place is bustling, it is full of busy activity
intersection *n.* （两条线的）相交；交点	an occasion when two lines cross, or the place where this happens
adjacent *adj.* 邻近的；毗连的	very near, next to, or touching
wholesale *adj.* 批发的；成批卖的	of or for the selling of goods in large amounts at low prices to shops and businesses, rather than the selling of goods in shops to customers
stupa *n.* 佛塔，浮图，浮屠	a building with a dome (= rounded roof), that is a holy place for Buddhists
enshrine *v.* 把……奉为神圣；珍藏	to contain or keep something as if in a holy place
disrepair *n.* 破败，失修	the state of being broken or old and needing to be repaired
mural *n.* 壁画	a large picture that has been painted on the wall of a room or building
executive *n.* （尤指商业机构中的）行政主管，经理	someone in a high position, especially in business, who makes decisions and puts them into action
erect *v.* 建立；建造	to build a building, wall, or other structure
excavate *v.* 发掘；挖出	to remove earth that is covering very old objects buried in the ground in order to discover things about the past
tribute *n.* （尤指在正式场合表达敬意的）颂词，礼物	something that you say, write, or give that shows your respect and admiration for someone, especially on a formal occasion

Notes and Explanations

➢ Jebumgang Lhakhang 吉崩岗拉康：西藏拉萨古城中心的历史建筑，现存唯一按坛城结构建造的古建筑。经当地文旅部门的抢救修复，"吉崩岗拉康"于2021年7月25日重新以"吉本岗艺术中心"呈现在公众面前，成为西藏首个古建筑保护性改造而成的文化艺术空间。

➢ Barkhor District 八廓街（八角街）：位于拉萨市城关区，是拉萨著名的转经道和商业中心，较完整地保存了古城的传统面貌和居住方式。八廓街原街道只是单一围绕大昭寺的转经道，藏族人称为"圣路"，现逐渐扩展为围绕大昭寺周围的大片旧式老街区。2023年11月，八廓街入选第三批国家级旅游休闲街区。

➢ National Cultural Relics Census 全国文物普查：国情国力调查的重要组成部分，文物普查对于促进文化遗产保护事业和经济社会发展具有重要意义，是提高文物保护队伍整体素质的重要机遇和提升全民文化遗产保护意识的重要手段。

Exercises

1. Dealing with Unfamiliar Words

Fill in the blanks in the following sentences with the correct form of the words and phrases from the box.

revival	keel	unevenness	fixture	texture
hurdle	peddler	dedicated	entrust	ingenuity
vitality	surveillance	carry out	cooperate with	flesh out

(1) This calculation illustrates the general _____ of the distribution of family responsibilities.

(2) The makers of this Yaozhou stoneware box carved four peony flowers into the leather-hard clay, added _____ using a comb tool, and then dipped the box into liquid glaze.

(3) We believe that hard work pays back and with great efforts comes national _____.

(4) These plans need to _____ with some more figures.

(5) On the basis of having project developers take responsibility for environmental protection while end-users assume responsibility for compensation, we need to look into setting up a _____ national fund for ecological compensation, and promote the establishment of a reserve fund system for the sustainable development of resource-based enterprises.

(6) In speech, it is not quantity but _____, not eloquence but insight, that counts.

(7) There has never been a greater need for us to understand, accommodate and _____ each other.

(8) Reform and opening-up is the path to making China strong. It provides powerful impetus for China's economic development, and is the source of _____ of the Party and the state.

(9) The amended Criminal Procedure Law adopted in 2012 stipulated that those criminals sentenced to public _____, probationary suspension, parole and serving terms outside of jail temporarily, should undergo community.

(10) Confucius believed that the superior should not be assigned trivial tasks, but _____ great undertakings.

2. Reading and Understanding

Decide whether the following statements are true (T) or false (F).

(1) Jebumgang was once a warehouse, a trading market and a cultural relic, but now an art center.

(2) The protection and renovation team gained inspiration from those successful cases from home and abroad.

(3) The floors and the columns were dismantled and replaced by the new ones for the sake of safety.

(4) Information technology has contributed to the renovation project, which has made it better known to people around the world.

(5) The success of Jebumgang Art Center not only sets an example for the renovation of the ancient architecture, but plays a vital role in the publicity of the distinctive culture.

3. Translating

Translate the following paragraph into Chinese.

Red is the life of southern Fujian architecture, with red walls, red tiles and red brick paving. It can be said that people in southern Fujian cannot live without red, which is an inseparable part of their lives. Taking local red clay as the main material, it is fired into red bricks and red tiles, which have become the unique visual characteristics of southern Fujian architecture. In addition to the most obvious regional characteristics of red buildings in Xiamen, Zhangzhou and Quanzhou, the ancient residential buildings in Putian area and in southern Fuqing area also belong to this kind of red architectural area.

4. Developing Critical Thinking

Work in pairs and discuss the following questions.

(1) Some people think that renovation of the cultural relics takes up the resources that can be used to help those in need. And it is much more meaningful than bringing the ancient architecture into life. So, what do you think of such renovation projects?

(2) In what way do you think can the advanced technology contribute to the conservation of Chinese traditional cultures, such as the ancient architecture, the Dunhuang Murals, and so on?

Further Reading

Tibetan Relics Show Solid Bonds Between Plateau and Plains

The Potala Palace, a landmark in southwest China's Tibet Autonomous Region, features a mural that illustrates a historic marriage between the Han and Tibetan ethnic groups.

The mural depicts ancient Tibetan officials standing in a row, holding their hands in front of their chests, to welcome Wencheng, a princess of the Tang Dynasty (618-907). The princess traveled to Tibet to marry Tibetan King Songtsen Gampo in the 7th century.

Similar to the mural, many other relics in Tibet have helped further uncover cultural communication and integration between the plateau region and the rest of China.

Evidence on the Wall

Murals depicting the marriage between Princess Wencheng and Songtsen Gampo were also found in the Samye Monastery, a famed Tibetan Buddhist temple in Shannan City, Tibet.

"Princess Wencheng brought new varieties of crops to Tibet, and also helped improve local livestock breeds," said Basang, a monk from the monastery. "She made outstanding contributions to the ethnic unity between Han and Tibetan people."

Built in the 8th century on the northern bank of the Yarlung Zangbo River, the Samye Monastery was listed as a key cultural heritage site under national-level protection in 1996. The temple itself is also a manifestation of cultural integration.

The first floor of the main hall, built with rocks, features a Tibetan architectural style. The second floor, on the other hand, uses bricks and wood in a Han style, said Basang, 64, adding that the murals and statues on each floor are also consistent with their respective styles.

The Shalu Monastery, built in 1087 in the city of Xigaze, is another example of a mix of different architectural styles.

The monastery combines traditional Tibetan architecture with cultural traits popular in the Yuan Dynasty (1271-1368). Notable design choices from this period include the hip-and-gable roof, also known as the Xieshan roof, blue glazed tiles, and patterns of the flying maid, lion, tiger and flowers on the roof ridge.

Losa Gyatso with the monastery's management committee said Drakpa Gyaltsen, head of the Shalu area during the Yuan Dynasty, presented himself with Emperor Renzong and was granted a gold imperial decree, a jade seal, as well as offerings including gold and silver.

"With the offerings from the emperor and many Han craftsmen invited here to build the monastery, the project has become a symbol for communication, exchanges, integration and unity of different ethnic groups," said Losa Gyatso.

In the Yuan Dynasty, the central government exercised jurisdiction and governance over Tibet.

Underground Findings

The earliest archaeological site identified at the heart of the Qinghai-Tibet Plateau so far is the Nwya Devu site, located 4,600 meters above sea level, in northern Tibet.

More than 4,000 stone artifacts, including blades, flakes, chunks and tools, have been recovered at the paleolithic site since 2016.

Scientific analysis showed that the site dated back some 40,000 to 30,000 years, said Dr. Zhang Xiaoling from the Institute of Vertebrate Paleontology and Paleoanthropology, Chinese Academy of Sciences, adding that it is also the highest paleolithic site in altitude ever found in the world so far.

Archaeological findings throughout Tibet's history have also provided abundant evidence to the cultural integration between the region and other areas.

For example, the wooden figurines unearthed from the Sangmda Lungga tomb site in Zanda County in Tibet's Ngari Prefecture are similar in shape to those found in the tombs in the neighboring Xinjiang Uygur Autonomous Region.

He Wei, an associate researcher with the regional cultural relics protection research institute, said the relics site spanning 366 BC to AD 668 witnessed political and economic development, integrating multiple cultures from the surrounding areas, such as those in Xinjiang and the plain areas in central China.

The cultural connection between Tibet and the Yellow River basin was proven at the Karub ruins in the city of Qamdo with the discovery of the millet, a crop customarily planted in northern China. The finding proved the communication between the plateau and northern China some 5,000 years ago.

Shaka Wangdu, a researcher with the regional cultural relics protection research institute, said since ancient times Tibet has been a region where cross-cultural concepts and traditions have met and jointly formed the colorful culture of the plateau.

(Source: http://english.scio.gov.cn/in-depth/2022-04/11/content_78158611.htm)

Unit 7

China's Arts and Crafts

Text A

Chinese Embroidery

Embroidery, a folk art with a long tradition, has an important position in the history of Chinese arts and crafts. In its long development embroidery has been inseparable from silkworm raising and silk reeling and weaving.

China was the first country in the world to weave silk. Silkworms were domesticated as early as some 5,000 years ago. The production of silk threads and fabrics gave rise to the art of embroidery. In 1958, a piece of silk embroidered with a dragon and phoenix was discovered in a state of Chu tomb of the Warring Sates Period (475-221 BC). More than 2,000 years old, it is the earliest piece of Chinese embroidery ever unearthed. Embroidery became widespread during the Han Dynasty (206 BC-AD 220) and many embroidered pieces discovered date back to that period.

Today, silk embroidery is practiced nearly all over China. The Four Famous Embroideries of China refer to the Xiang embroidery in central China's Hunan Province, Shu embroidery in western China's Sichuan Province, Yue embroidery in southern China's Guangdong Province and Su embroidery in eastern China's Jiangsu Province.

Xiang Embroider

Xiang embroidery is well known for its time-honored history, excellent craftsmanship and unique style. The earliest piece of Xiang embroidery was unearthed at the No.1 Tomb of Mawangdui, Changsha City of the Han Dynasty (206 BC-AD 220). The weaving technique was almost the same as the one used in modern times, which demonstrated that embroidery had already existed in the Han Dynasty. In its later development, Xiang Embroidery absorbed the characteristics of traditional Chinese paintings and formed its own unique characteristics. Xiang embroidery experienced its heyday at the end of the Qing Dynasty (1644-1911) and in the early Republic of China (early 20th century), even surpassing Su embroidery. After the founding of the People's Republic of China, Xiang embroidery was further improved and developed to a new level.

Xiang embroidery uses pure silk, hard satin, soft satin and nylon as its material, which is connected with colorful silk threads. Absorbing the spirit of Chinese paintings, the embroidery reaches a high artistic level. Xiang embroidery crafts include valuable works of art, as well as materials for daily use.

Shu Embroidery

Also called Chuan embroidery, Shu embroidery is the general name for embroidery products in areas around Chengdu, Sichuan Province. Shu embroidery enjoys a long history. As early as the Han Dynasty, Shu embroidery was already famous. The central government even designated an office in this area for its administration. During the Five Dynasties and Ten States periods (907-960), a peaceful society and large demand provided advanced conditions for the rapid development of the Shu Embroidery industry. Shu embroidery experienced its peak development in the Song Dynasty (960-1279), ranking first in both production and excellence. In the mid-Qing Dynasty, the Shu embroidery industry was formed. After the founding of the People's Republic of China, Shu embroidery factories were set up and the craft entered a new phase of development, using innovative techniques and a larger variety of forms.

Originating among the folk people in the west of Sichuan Province, Shu embroidery formed its own unique characteristics: smooth, bright, neat and influenced by the geographical environment, customs and cultures. The works incorporated flowers, leaves, animals, mountains, rivers and human figures as their themes. Altogether, there are 122 approaches in 12 categories for weaving. The craftsmanship of Shu embroidery involves a combination of fine arts, aesthetics and practical uses, such as the facings of quits, pillowcases, coats, shoots and screen covers.

Yue Embroidery

Yue embroidery, also called Guang embroidery, is a general name for embroidery products of the regions of Guangzhou, Shantou, Zhongshan, Panyu and Shunde in Guangdong Province. According to historical records, in the first year of Yongzhen's reign (805) during the Tang Dynasty (618-907), a girl named Lu Meiniang embroidered the seventh volume of the Fahua Buddhist Scripture on a piece of thin silk 30 cm long. And so, Yue embroidery became famous around the country. The prosperous Guangzhou Port of the Song Dynasty promoted the development of Yue embroidery, which began to be exported at that time. During Qianlong's reign (1736-1796) of the Qing, an industrial organization was established in Guangzhou. At that time, a large number of craftsmen devoted themselves to the craft, inciting further improvements to the weaving technique. Since 1915, the work of

Yue embroidery garnered several awards at the Panama Expo.

Influenced by national folk art, Yue embroidery formed its own unique characteristics. The embroidered pictures are mainly of dragons and phoenixes, and flowers and birds, with neat designs and strong, contrasting colors. Floss, thread and gold-and-silk thread embroidery are used to produce costumes, decorations for halls and crafts for daily use.

Su Embroidery

With a history of more than 3,000 years, Su embroidery is the general name for embroidery products in areas around Suzhou, Jiangsu Province. The craft, which dates back to the Three Kingdoms Period (220−280), became a sideline of people in the Suzhou area during the Ming Dynasty (1368−1644). Well known for its smoothness and delicateness, Su embroidery won Suzhou the title City of Embroidery in the Qing Dynasty. In the mid and late Qing, Su embroidery experienced further developments involving works of double-sided embroidering. There were 65 embroidery stores in Suzhou City. During the Republic of China period (1912−1949), the Su embroidery industry was in decline due to frequent wars and it was restored and regenerated after the founding of the People's Republic of China. In 1950, the central government set up research centers for Su embroidery and launched training courses for the study of embroidery. Weaving methods have climbed from 18 to the present 40.

Su embroidery features a strong, folk flavor and its weaving techniques are characterized by the following: the product surface must be flat, the rim must be neat, the needle must be thin, the lines must be dense, the color must be harmonious and bright and the picture must be even. Su embroidery products fall into three major categories: costumes, decorations for halls and crafts for daily use, which integrate decorative and practical values. Double-sided embroidery is an excellent representative of Su embroidery.

In addition to the four major embroidery styles there are Ou embroidery of Wenzhou, Zhejiang Province; Bian embroidery of Kaifeng, Henan Province and Han embroidery of Wuhan, Hubei Province.

(Source: http://en.chinaculture.org/library/2008-01/22/content_45156.htm)

Language Focus

Words and Expressions

embroidery *n.* 刺绣；绣花	patterns that are sewn onto cloth using threads of various colors; cloth that is decorated in this way
inseparable *adj.* （与某事物）分不开的；形影不离的	not able to be separated
domesticate *v.* 驯养，驯化（动物）	to make a wild animal used to living with or working for humans
phoenix *n.* 凤凰；（传说中的）长生鸟	(in stories) a magic bird that lives for several hundred years before burning itself and then being born again from its ashes
tomb *n.* 坟墓；冢	a large grave, especially one built of stone above or below the ground
unearth *v.* 使出土；（偶然或经搜寻）发现，找到；发掘；挖掘	to find something in the ground by digging; to find or discover something by chance or after searching for it
heyday *n.* 最为强大（或成功、繁荣）的时期	the time when somebody/something had most power or success, or was most popular
satin *n.* 缎子	a type of cloth with a smooth shiny surface
innovative *adj.* 创新的；革新的	introducing or using new ideas, ways of doing something, etc.
originate *v.* 起源；创建	to happen or appear for the first time in a particular place or situation
scripture *n.* 经文；（某宗教的）圣典，经典	the holy books of a particular religion
incite *v.* 煽动；鼓动	to encourage somebody to do something violent, illegal or unpleasant, especially by making them angry or excited

93

sideline *n.* 兼职；副业；兼营业务	an activity that you do as well as your main job in order to earn extra money
regenerate *v.* 使振兴；发展壮大	to make an area, institution, etc. develop and grow strong again

Notes and Explanations

➤ double-sided embroidery 双面绣：中国优秀的民族传统工艺之一。双面绣始于宋代，是在同一块底料上，在同一绣制过程中，绣出正反两面图像，其轮廓完全一样，图案同样精美，均可供人仔细欣赏。

Exercises

1. Dealing with Unfamiliar Words
   Match the words in the left with their definitions.

   (1) garner   the level of skill shown by somebody in making something beautiful with their hands

   (2) fabrics   to satisfy someone by giving them something that is wanted or needed

   (3) intangible   the outer, often curved or circular, edge of something

   (4) craftsmanship   to collect something, usually after much work or with difficulty

   (5) sate   cloth or material for making clothes, covering furniture, etc.

   (6) dissolution   the act or process of ending an official organization or legal agreement

   (7) rim   that exists but that is difficult to describe, understand or measure

   (8) innovation   the introduction of new things, ideas or ways of doing something

2. Reading and Understanding
   Decide whether the following statements are true (T) or false (F).

   (1) Silk embroidery plays a vital role in Chinese history and is merely practiced in Hunan, Sichuan, Guangdong and Jiangsu.

   (2) The uniqueness of Xiang embroidery lies in its reference to Chinese traditional paintings.

   (3) Shu embroidery has not been industrialized until the founding of the People's Republic of China.

   (4) Yue embroidery is inspired by Chinese folk art and enjoys a great reputation from

home and abroad.

(5) Xiang embroidery, Shu embroidery, Yue embroidery and Su embroidery mentioned in the text have both aesthetics and practical value.

3. Questions for Discussion

   Work in small groups and discuss the following questions.

   (1) In addition to silk embroidery, what other kind of Chinese traditional art do you know?

   (2) Do you think we should spend time and money for the conservation of silk embroidery in the 21st century? Why or why not?

   (3) The process of modernization has challenged the position of Chinese traditional art. What do you think of the traditional culture in modern time?

4. Translating

   Translate the following paragraph into English.

   中国的新型文明观根植于中国传统文化，尤其是传统和合文化，其出发点与落脚点与文明冲突论截然不同。中国倡导树立平等、互鉴、对话、包容的文明观，尊重世界文明多样性，以文明交流超越文明隔阂，文明互鉴超越文明冲突，文明共存超越文明优越，深化文明交流互鉴，促进各国人民相知相亲，共同应对各种全球性挑战。每一个国家和民族的文明都扎根于本国本民族的土壤之中，都有自己的本色、长处、优点，应该维护各国各民族文明多样性，加强相互交流、相互学习、相互借鉴，而不应该相互隔膜、相互排斥、相互取代，这样世界文明之园才能万紫千红、生机盎然。

Text B

Calligraphy, the Gem of Chinese Culture

Calligraphy is something very special for Chinese. It is not only an important part of traditional Chinese culture but also a way of life for people of all stripes.

Like oil painting and sculpture in the West, calligraphy is as much an artistic form as a spiritual anchor for many Chinese throughout history. Rarely does any other culture in human history fascinate with calligraphy in such a profound way.

From the invention of hieroglyphics to the evolution of various calligraphic scripts, calligraphy has played a critical role in Chinese culture and history for thousands of years.

Calligraphy was well-respected, or even worshiped in history. It was a foundation for scarcely available education opportunities, a steppingstone to become the elite class and a prerequisite for admiration among peers. In essence, calligraphy is also the cultural identity and the manifestation of collective aesthetic philosophy.

During Jin Dynasty (266–420), calligraphy became an expression of superiority among noble families. The rivalries were so intense that young children were ordered to receive extensive training in calligraphy.

Wang Xizhi was among those raised in noble families. Along with his son, Wang Xianzhi, the Wangs were considered the greatest calligraphers in Chinese history whose achievements were insurmountable for late generations. Therefore, Jin Dynasty is the pinnacle of calligraphic works in Chinese history.

However, calligraphy inevitably intersected with politics in Chinese history. In Tang Dynasty (618–907), the Emperor Taizong not only revered Wang Xizhi's calligraphy, but himself was also good at it. He considered Wang Xizhi as the greatest calligrapher in history. His obsession with Wang Xizhi made him promote his subordinates based on their talents to mimic Wang's works.

Above all, the emperor regarded the *Preface to the Orchid Pavilion Collection* by Wang Xizhi as the best running script. Prized as his priceless treasure, the emperor kept Wang's works only for his most trusted subordinates and, after his death, he was buried along with Wang's works.

It was understood that calligraphy became one piece of matrices for the emperor to seek loyalty, unity and capability among his subordinates. Not surprisingly, Tang Dynasty was another Golden Age of Chinese calligraphy. A generation of great calligraphers, such as Ouyang Xun, Yu Shinan, Chu Suiliang, Yan Zhenqing, Sun Guoting, Liu Gongquan and many others, emerged whose calligraphic works also became masterpieces for later generations to emulate.

Calligraphy in ancient China was critically important for Chinese literati. Since the practice of the imperial examination, calligraphic skill may change the fate of those examinees. It was generalized that, since so few were able to receive formal education, their intercultural ability and their qualification to serve the emperors correlated with calligraphy.

Moreover, the examiners might not have enough time to go through all the essays, and they tended to rank candidates based on calligraphy rather than contents. Therefore, calligraphy somewhat became a strong indicator for talent and promotion.

Even in daily lives, people with calligraphic skills were highly respected and in high demand for letters, contracts, Buddhist scriptures, as well as decorations for weddings and funerals.

Nowadays, *zhongtang*, which consists of three pieces of calligraphic works and a water-color painting, is the most elegant feature of the living room and is still popular in rural areas of northwestern China.

It is a meticulous plan to set up the *zhongtang* in order to impress the guests. The choice of calligraphy and, most importantly, its meaning reflects the social status in the neighborhood and is considered as one of the most important assets for fortune and prosperity for generations.

Although urbanization offers limited space required for traditional *zhongtang*, it is still a common practice for many to assemble calligraphic works in the living rooms. In modern China, calligraphy in such formats as mottos has emerged as an expression of aesthetic philosophy and personality.

Calligraphy used to be a privilege among the well-educated elites. Nowadays, significant reduction in poverty and illiteracy encourages more and more people to practice calligraphy. As much as recreation, physical fitness and artistic appreciation, calligraphy is becoming a part of life among many Chinese people. With numerous calligraphy training courses and interest groups among local schools and communities, plus various calligraphic competitions, exhibitions and auctions, today is another golden age of Chinese calligraphy.

(Source: http://en.chinaculture.org/2018-03/21/content_1172587.htm)

Language Focus

Words and Expressions

stripe *n.* 条纹，斑纹	a strip on the surface of something that is a different colour from the surrounding surface
hieroglyphics *n.* 象形文字（尤指古埃及的文字）	a system of writing that uses pictures instead of words, especially as used in ancient Egypt
evolution *n.* 演化；进化	the way in which living things change and develop over millions of years
prerequisite *n.* 先决条件，前提，必备条件	something that must exist or happen before something else can exist or happen
manifestation *n.* 显示；表明	a sign of something existing or happening
insurmountable *adj.* （尤指问题或困难）难以克服的，不可逾越的	(especially of a problem or a difficulty) so great that it cannot be dealt with successfully
pinnacle *n.* 极点；顶点，顶峰	the most successful or admired part of a system or achievement
intersect *v.* （线条、道路等）（和……）相交，（和……）交叉	(of lines, roads, etc.) to cross one another
revere *v.* 尊敬；崇敬	to very much respect and admire someone or something
obsession *n.* 困扰；无法摆脱的念头；念念不忘的事（或人）	something or someone that you think about all the time
subordinate *adj.* 从属的，下级的；次要的	having a lower or less important position
mimic *v.* （为逗乐而）模仿，学……的样子	to copy the way in which a particular person usually speaks and moves, usually in order to make people laugh

matrix　*n.* （事物成长发展的）条件，环境（matrices 的单数）	the set of conditions that provides a system in which something grows or develops
unity　*n.* 联合；一致；团结；和睦	the state of being joined together or in agreement
literati　*n.* 文人，学士	people with a good education who know a lot about literature

Notes and Explanations

➢ *Preface to the Orchid Pavilion Collection*《兰亭集序》：晋朝（266—420）"书圣"王羲之写出的"天下第一行书"。《兰亭集序》记述的是王羲之和友人雅士会聚兰亭（今浙江省绍兴市兰亭镇）盛游之事，其书从容娴和，气盛神凝。

Exercises

1. Dealing with Unfamiliar Words

   Fill in the blanks in the following sentences with the correct form of the words and phrases from the box.

meticulous	insurmountable	prosperity	urbanization	aesthetic
privilege	correlate	illiteracy	recreational	auction
pinnacle	poverty	set up	tend to	in demand

   (1) A country's future _____ depends, to an extent, upon the quality of education of its people.

   (2) For Kautsky, the mass strike was never more than a defensive weapon only to be used in the last resort if the democratic _____ of the working class were attacked.

   (3) Many hours of _____ preparation have gone into writing the book.

   (4) This small country is faced with an _____ debt.

   (5) By the age of 32 she had reached the _____ of her career.

   (6) Teachers and other professionals are taking part in a campaign to eradicate _____.

   (7) Consumer spending was promoted in key areas, spurring rapid growth in spending on _____ travel, online shopping, and information goods and services.

   (8) People _____ think that the problem will never affect them.

(9) The family is _____ (off) its art collection.

(10) In addition, the expressionist oil paintings fused with Chinese traditional spirit of art show a new _____ characteristic.

2. Reading and Understanding

Decide whether the following statements are true (T) or false (F).

(1) Calligraphy, in ancient China, has once become a recreation of the upper class and a symbol of their superiority.

(2) The examiners in ancient China ranked examinees based on their calligraphy and content.

(3) Calligraphy was once regarded as a tie between literati and emperors.

(4) Calligraphers practiced their skills merely for promotion and political pursuit in their career.

(5) The publicity of calligraphy has gained a great success in modern China due to the improvement of people's living hood.

3. Translating

Translate the following paragraph into Chinese.

Promoting exchanges and mutual learning among civilizations is China's basic stance on dealing with inter-civilizational relations. Diversity spurs exchanges among civilizations, which in turn promote mutual learning and their further development. This embodies China's new concept of civilization. A sign of social development and progress, civilizations also represent the ideas and values of different societies. Therefore, civilizations are naturally diverse rather than monotonous.

4. Developing Critical Thinking

Work in pairs and discuss the following questions.

(1) How do you understand the title of the text? In what way calligraphy represents the gem of Chinese culture?

(2) How do you think of the publicity of Chinese traditional culture in modern society, such as calligraphy, martial arts and so on?

Further Reading

China Focus: Shipwreck Archaeology Unveils Glory of Maritime Silk Road

More than 700 years ago, a vessel loaded with porcelains sank off the coast of east China's Fujian Province while en route overseas.

The underwater wreckage near the islet of Shengbeiyu in the city of Zhangzhou was recently unveiled in an archaeological salvage project, presenting to the world the historical prosperity of the Maritime Silk Road during that era.

The salvage, which kicked off in September last year and lasted until this month, was jointly conducted by the National Centre of Archaeology (NCA), the Fujian Provincial Research Institute of Archaeology and the Zhangzhou Municipal Bureau of Culture and Tourism.

Located at the intersection of the eastern route and the southern route of the ancient Maritime Silk Road, the sea waters near the Shengbeiyu islet is a shipwreck-prone area as it is surrounded by reefs and has complex sea conditions.

The ship from the Yuan Dynasty (1271-1368) was found there under the sediment at a water depth of about 30 meters.

Nearly 20,000 items have been retrieved, with the collection comprising over 17,100 Longquan Celadon porcelains, renowned in China for their exquisite colors, particularly the shades of jade green and light blue. Bowls, plates, cups and incense burners are among the retrieved porcelains, which are believed to have been produced in the late Yuan Dynasty.

"The sunken ship contains the largest number of Longquan porcelains found onboard to date, serving as a typical example of the Longquan porcelain exports peak of the late Yuan Dynasty," said Chen Hao, deputy head of the underwater archaeology center of the Fujian Provincial Research Institute of Archaeology.

Some porcelains were engraved with characters, such as "Yong" "Bao" and "Nian," meaning "use" "treasure" and "year" respectively. These porcelains have become important materials for research on the export of Longquan porcelains, Chen said at a press conference held earlier this month.

According to Chen, the discovery also ascertains that the government back then encouraged overseas trade, making the Maritime Silk Road especially prosperous in the Yuan Dynasty.

Among the porcelains found were giant plates with a diameter of 35 cm and a height of

4.3 cm, rarely seen in China.

Liu Miao, an associate professor at Xiamen University, said the big plates were produced based on overseas dining customs, an apparent customized design for porcelain exports.

Combining the archaeological findings at an ancient port in the city of Wenzhou in Zhejiang Province and the high similarity between archaeological discoveries of the sunken ship and the porcelains excavated in Southeast Asia, experts assume that it was a civil merchant ship setting off from the port of Wenzhou to Southeast Asia.

The salvage project team for the first time adopted underwater photographic stitching to obtain a panoramic high-definition three-dimensional image of the wreck site in low visibility sea conditions.

Liang Guoqing, the team leader who works with the NCA, said they previously thought the ship had seven cabins. However, as the dredging work went on, they found it had 10 cabins, indicating that it was a large merchant ship for trade.

Liang added that the salvage project involving the sunken ship is a milestone in China's underwater archaeology history.

"The discovery has enabled people to get a glimpse of the booming trade of Longquan Celadon porcelains as well as the prosperity of the Maritime Silk Road," he said.

(Source: https://english.news.cn/20231031/bc7efb0269f64cf8a183b811e52d70a7/c.html)

Unit 8

China's Customs and Festivals

Text A

Chinese Festival Going Global with Dragon Boats

The Dragon Boat Festival was celebrated among overseas Chinese communities worldwide over the weekend with the specialty food Zongzi, but not necessarily a dragon boat race, both widely seen as its logos.

Dragon boat racing is officially a competitive sport played under rules set by the International Dragon Boat Federation. This is something beyond what the Chinese people could imagine some 2,500 years ago when they took boats to distribute feed in a river trying to keep fish from disturbing the permanent rest of patriotic and beloved poet Qu Yuan, who chose to die along with his doomed country.

The move inspired a water sport and a rice food, and accidentally, changed the face and the name to be known abroad of an old Chinese festival focusing on health and epidemic prevention — the 5th day of the 5th month of a Chinese lunar year which coincidentally marks the death anniversary of Qu.

A Sport That Has Gone Global

The Dragon Boat Festival this year fell on June 18. However, a dragon boat race nowadays takes place any time in a year in several countries. It is one of Britain's fastest growing water sport as well as a highlight in London's cultural calendar. On June 3, the 23rd edition of the annual London Hong Kong Dragon Boat Festival entertained 10,000 visitors. Hundreds of players, among them teenagers, elders, amateurs and corporate employees, of 33 teams from across Britain paddled vigorously to the beat of each team's own drum and amid stormy cheers from the bank, competing for six cups at London's Regatta Center.

"I have never, ever experienced anything like it. I think it is amazing. I found it is really interesting, but honestly, I do not know much about it," Stephanie Ann, a local visitor coming with her family, told Xinhua.

On the sidelines, live music, traditional Chinese lion dances, and an Asian food market are among the diverse cultural activities contributing to the biggest dragon boat races in Europe. In the United States, dragon boat racing is popular in cities including San Francisco, Kansas City and Boston. In New York City, it has become the largest local summer event.

The 28th annual Hong Kong Dragon Boat Festival in New York is scheduled for Aug. 11–12, and more than 200 well-trained teams will participate. "I'm captain and drummer, we have a new steerer this year and we are moving into using the fiber glass boats instead of the timber boats for the race," Julia Chesler told Xinhua after a three-hour team training recently on the Meadow Lake, the race venue.

A Festival Goes Further with Dragon Boats

Still, somewhere, the old-fashioned dragon-headed boats strongly suggest a cultural background, indicating a close link of the sport with China. "It was quite a good experience...I will remember it because it is something we associate with Chinese culture," said Din Musovic, a high school student of the champion team from the June 9 race held in Croatia's capital Zagreb to mark the upcoming Dragon Boat Festival. At least, the dragon boat's unique shape is eye-catching. On Saturday, a dragon boat sailed in a canal running through downtown Aveiro in northern Portugal, interesting many people.

The sailing proved to be the most dramatic part of the local Dragon Boat Festival celebrations. City official Catarina Barreto praised the celebrations co-hosted by the Confucius Institute at the University of Aveiro, saying they brought together the traditional cultures of Portugal and China and called for more.

Uganda saw the 2nd edition of its Dragon Boat Festival on Saturday on the shore of Lake Victoria. It turned out to be a big event with barbecues, kite flying, live music, Chinese and Ugandan food, performances of Chinese waist drums and Ugandan folk dance. Its opening ceremony was attended by Uganda's Vice President Edward Kiwanuka Ssekandi and a visiting Chinese official. "I'm sure this Dragon Boat Festival will be an avenue to make Ugandans and Chinese (migrants) live more happily together and cooperate better," Ssekandi said, adding that the dragon boat race integrated elements of the two countries' traditional cultures.

Addressing the opening ceremony, Wang Yang, chairman of the National Committee of the Chinese People's Political Consultative Conference, said dragon boat racing embodies traditional Chinese values such as mutual benefit, seeking harmony in diversity, and working in unity and cooperation.

Family-made Zongzi

Traditional Chinese festivals can always be tasted, and the Dragon Boat Festival is no exception. Zongzi, a glutinous rice dumpling wrapped in bamboo or reed leaves in cone- or pyramid-like shapes, is the special treat and delicacy on the festival table. It was purely good luck that led Frank, a German visitor who only gave his first name, into Lao Sze Chuan in downtown Chicago on Sunday, who ordered for friends a debuted special offer by the Chinese restaurant.

It was a Zongzi stuffed with pork and duck egg yolk amid rice. "It's really a good combination of flavors, I really enjoyed it... It's worth a shot," he commented. "I was actually quite surprised."

The restaurant said guests consumed more than 280 pieces of Zongzi in less than three hours. But for Richard Hennessy, it was more than a pleasing dining experience — he took the invitation to make Zongzi with the help of cooks.

Hennessy believed the Zongzi he made was the star of the night. "It's a great fun. Now we can go home and practice some more," he said.

Although modern life facilitations enable the Zongzi made in China to be only a few clicks away, restaurant owner Tony Hu plans to make Zongzi-making a Dragon Boat Festival routine. "Chinese food is the easiest way for them to know China, and cut short their distance with Chinese people," said Hu.

Zongzi has been a food mostly family-made in China, and many Chinese learn the knacks of making it from their parents. It is a good example to show traditional Chinese values — the cooking activity calls for collaboration among family members, with its results shared by all.

For many Chinese, making Zongzi never fails to evoke a feeling of being at home.

"On a festival like this, we want to help with the homesickness of Chinese living abroad, and introduce traditional Chinese culture to people here," said Zuqi Su, co-owner of Chinese restaurant Jasmine in downtown Manhattan, New York, which offered a Zongzi making workshop on Saturday and Sunday.

Anirudh Singh did his homework on Chinese culture before participating in the restaurant's Dragon Boat Festival celebration. "The fishermen threw rice in the river to make sure the fish didn't eat Qu Yuan's body, right?" he said. "I learnt all about it before I came here."

Do It Yourself was partly why the workshop charmed Thomas Hasler, an Austrian among the more than 100 participants. "I enjoy this so much," he said. "I eat out a lot at Chinese restaurants, but being able to make something has been so much more fun."

(Source: http://english.scio.gov.cn/in-depth/2018-06/19/content_52671684.htm)

Language Focus

Words and Expressions

patriotic *adj.* 爱国的	showing love for your country and being proud of it
beloved *adj.* 挚爱的；深受爱戴的	loved very much
doomed *adj.* 命定的；注定要失败的	certain to fail, die, or be destroyed
coincidentally *adv.* 巧合地	because of chance or luck
paddle *v.* 用桨划船	to push a pole with a wide end through the water in order to make a boat move
vigorously *adv.* 精神旺盛地，有力地	in a way that is very forceful or energetic
regatta *n.* 赛艇会，划船比赛	a sports event consisting of boat races
sideline *n.* 两侧场外区域	a line that shows the position of the side of an area where a sport is played
timber *n.* 木材	a long piece of wood used for building, especially houses and ships
migrant *n.* （为工作）移居者，移民	a person that travels to a different country or place, often in order to find work
glutinous *adj.* 黏的，胶质的	sticky
delicacy *n.* 美味，佳肴	something especially rare or expensive that is good to eat
knack *n.* 技能；本领	a skill or an ability to do something easily and well
collaboration *n.* 合作，协作	the situation of two or more people working together to create or achieve the same thing

Notes and Explanations

➤ The Confucius Institute 孔子学院：推广汉语和传播中国文化的非营利教育机构，由外方机构自愿申请，中外合作方本着相互尊重、友好协商、平等互利原则设立，一般下设于国外的大学和研究院等教育机构中。孔子学院旨在促进中文国际传播，加深世界人民对中国语言文化的了解，增进中外教育人文交流。

➤ The National Committee of the Chinese People's Political Consultative Conference 中国人民政治协商会议全国委员会（简称"政协全国委员会"或"全国政协"）：由中国共产党、各民主党派、无党派人士、人民团体、各少数民族和各界的代表，香港特别行政区同胞、澳门特别行政区同胞、台湾同胞和归国侨胞的代表以及特别邀请的人士组成，每届任期5年。

Exercises

1. Dealing with Unfamiliar Words

   Match the words in the left with their definitions.

   (1) regatta   a person that travels to a different country, often in order to find work

   (2) delicacy   a long piece of wood used for building, especially houses and ships

   (3) migrant   a sports event consisting of boat races

   (4) timber   something especially rare or expensive that is good to eat

   (5) knack   the situation of two or more people working together to create or achieve the same thing

   (6) collaboration   a skill or an ability to do something easily and well

   (7) paddle   a line that shows the position of the side of an area where a sport is played

   (8) sideline   to push a pole with a wide end through the water in order to make a boat move

2. Reading and Understanding

   Decide whether the following statements are true (T) or false (F).

   (1) Other countries also follow traditional Chinese calendar to hold dragon boat races.

   (2) Dragon boat race has become the fastest growing water sport in the UK.

   (3) In some cities of America, dragon boat racing has become the largest local seasonal event.

   (4) According to the passage, every traditional Chinese festival boasts a delicacy.

(5) Before participating the celebration about Dragon Boat Festival, Anirudh Singh did his homework assigned by school first.

3. Questions for Discussion

Work in small groups and discuss the following questions.

(1) Why dragon boat racing is popular worldwide?

(2) To promote traditional Chinese culture, what experience can we draw from the global popularity of Dragon Boat Festival?

(3) What is indicated in "Traditional Chinese festivals can always be tasted"? Please give as many examples as you can to illustrate this sentence.

4. Translating

Translate the following paragraph into English.

在古代，端午节处于疾病比较流行的夏初。艾叶作为草药被用于对抗这些疾病，其香味可以驱赶苍蝇和蚊子。菖蒲是一种水生植物，具有类似的效果。在农历五月初五，人们通常会打扫房屋和庭院，并在门楣上悬挂艾草和菖蒲，以预防疾病。也有人说挂艾草和菖蒲能给家庭带来好运。

Unit 8 China's Customs and Festivals

Text B

Customs Around the Mid-Autumn Festival

The traditional Mid-Autumn Festival enjoys great popularity in China where it is second only to the Spring Festival, or Chinese New Year, and in some of its neighboring countries.

The Mid-Autumn Festival falls on the 15th day of the eighth lunar month. Since ancient times, people have celebrated it by worshipping and admiring the glorious full moon, and enjoying osmanthus flowers and fermented-osmanthus wine. The Chinese believe that the full moon represents family reunions. Therefore, Mid-Autumn Festival is also a day for families to get together and for those far away from home to think of their loved ones.

Influenced by Chinese culture, certain other countries in East and Southeast Asia also celebrate the Mid-Autumn Festival. In 2006, the holiday was added to the list of China's first batch of national intangible cultural heritages.

Origins

Mid-Autumn Day, as the name suggests, usually falls in late September. As the full moon implies family reunions, it is also called the "reunion festival."

The Chinese people's tradition of worshiping the moon and offering sacrifices to it can be traced back more than 2,000 years. The Mid-Autumn Festival also happens to be a harvest season. To show their gratitude to Heaven for a good harvest, Chinese ancients held celebratory activities around this day. At this time of year, it's cool, but not yet cold. Clear skies and crisp air make it a good time to enjoy the beauty of the full moon. Hence, later, celebrations of the festival laid greater emphasis on enjoying the moon rather than making sacrifices, as new connotations became attached to it.

Ancient customs, rites, myths, legends and other factors of traditional Chinese culture have combined to imbue the Mid-Autumn Festival with rich content and cultural connotations in its evolution. The most famous legends told around the festival are fairy tales about the Moon Palace, relating to such figures as the Moon Goddess, and Tang Dynasty Emperor Li Longji (685–762) and his concubine Yang Yuhuan.

In the seventh century, the Mid-Autumn became an established festival as related celebrations of a bright full moon and feasting became prevalent. In the 10th century, the mooncake, a special dessert for the day, made an appearance, and the festival became even more popular as the accompanying celebrations evolved. By the 14th century, its importance was second only to that of the Spring Festival.

At Mid-Autumn Festival, a memorial tablet to the Moon Goddess is set up in each household with fruits, melons and mooncakes placed in front of it as a sacrifice. The cake must be round and melons and fruits cut into lotus-petal-shaped pieces. Some people also buy joss paper with images of the Goddess and patterns like the Jade Rabbit making heavenly medicine printed on it. After the moon-worshipping ceremony, people burn the joss paper and family members share the fruits and moon cakes. At the festival of family reunion, people give each other mooncakes as gifts to express their good wishes.

Apart from the common traditions, different regions also have their unique customs and celebrations on this day. For people in East China's Zhejiang Province, tidal bore watching is an important event on this day when the Earth is at its almost closest position to the Sun, when the most spectacular tides are formed in the Qiantang River. Its turbulent waves can sometimes reach several meters in height, overwhelming everything in their way, like herds of stampeding horses.

One particular Chinese folk tale relates how in the Moon Palace there was a huge osmanthus tree, more than 1,000 meters tall. Due to his violation of Taoist rules, Wu Gang was banished to the Moon Palace to cut down the tree as punishment. However, the sacred tree could self-heal the cuts Wu made on its trunk. Although hundreds of years passed by, the magic tree still thrived even though Wu chopped it diligently every day. Wu was allowed to rest only on the Mid-Autumn Day.

The eighth month of the lunar calendar is also a season of osmanthus blossom fragrance. Blossoms can be used to make various delicacies. It has therefore become traditional for people to drink fermented wine made from osmanthus flowers on that day, while eating other osmanthus-flavored delicacies.

In Guangzhou, on Mid-Autumn night, kids fix different shaped lanterns on short sticks that are then positioned vertically one by one on a high pole. These splendidly glittering lights, add a new beauty to the festival. Kids enjoy racing to be the first to erect the highest pole hung with the most exquisite and largest number of lamps. In Nanning, Guangxi Zhuang Autonomous Region, people also have a tradition of making lamps with bamboo strips that are hung in front of a moon-worshipping table. Kids also play with these lamps. In addition, lamps made from grapefruit and orange peel are also popular during this festival.

(Source: http://www.chinatoday.com.cn/english/culture/2016-08/31/content_726986.htm)

Language Focus

Words and Expressions

worship v. 崇拜；献祭	show devotion to (a deity); attend religious services
gratitude n. 感激，感谢，感恩	a feeling of thankfulness and appreciation
crisp adj. 清爽的；秋高气爽的	pleasantly cold and invigorating
connotation n. 内涵；含义	a quality or an idea that a word makes you think of that is more than its basic meaning
rite n. 仪式	an established ceremony prescribed by a religion
feast n. 盛宴，筵席；宴会	a large meal where a lot of people celebrate a special occasion
turbulent adj. 湍流的，湍急的	turbulent water or air contains strong currents which change direction suddenly
overwhelm v. 淹没	cover completely and usually suddenly
sacred adj. 神圣的	worthy of respect or dedication
thrive v. 繁盛；繁荣；成长	grow vigorously; make steady progress
diligent adj. 勤勉的；坚持不懈的	characterized by care and perseverance in carrying out tasks
vertical adj. 垂直的	perpendicular to the plane of the horizon or to a primary axis
exquisite adj. 精致的，精美的	extremely beautiful and very delicately made

Notes and Explanations

➤ **Mid-Autumn Festival 中秋节**：农历八月十五，中国的传统节日之一。据说源于远古的祭月崇拜。《礼记》曰："天子春朝日，秋夕月。朝日以朝，夕月以夕。""夕月以夕"就是指夜晚祭祀月亮。唐代，八月十五被定为一个节日，祭月变成了赏月，并增加了"团圆"的内涵。宋代，中秋节极为兴盛，成为重大的节日，这一天人们可以通宵达旦地游玩。元代末年，又出现了吃月饼的习俗。明代末年，北方一些地区又出现祭祀兔儿爷的习俗。

➤ **Moon Palace 广寒宫，蟾宫，月宫**：中国古代神话中对月亮上的宫殿的称呼，传说广寒宫中住有嫦娥、玉兔和吴刚。

➤ **Moon Goddess 嫦娥**：原称恒我、姮娥，是中国神话人物，为后羿之妻。嫦娥奔月是中国古代神话传说，相传嫦娥为了保持年轻美貌，遂偷食西王母赐予后羿的长生不老神药而奔月。

➤ **Wu Gang 吴刚**：中国神话人物。吴刚伐桂是中国古代神话传说，相传吴刚犯了天规受玉帝惩罚到月宫砍伐桂树，但桂树随砍随合，玉帝把这种永无休止的劳动作为对吴刚的惩罚。

Exercises

1. **Dealing with Unfamiliar Words**

   Fill in the blanks in the following sentences with the correct form of the words from the box.

feast	connotation	delicacy	sacred	illuminate
turbulence	crisp	exquisite	rite	overwhelm
thrive	gratitude	diligent	vertical	worship

   (1) The word "professional" has _____ of skill and excellence.

   (2) For a moment the scene was _____, then it was plunged back into darkness.

   (3) Small island states face the danger of being _____ as a result of climate change.

   (4) Life starts all over again when it gets _____ in the fall.

   (5) The dress shows an _____ design on its fine embroidery.

   (6) Few creatures are able to _____ in this grim and hostile land.

   (7) The king hosted a _____ in honor of his daughter's wedding, inviting all the nobles and dignitaries from neighboring kingdoms.

   (8) The world economy is facing _____ and uncertainty.

(9) The inhabitants _____ the sun, moon, mountains, rivers, forests and other natural phenomena including fire.

(10) Tourists will have opportunities to enjoy Chinese opera and acrobatic shows and taste authentic Chinese food and local _____.

2. Reading and Understanding

Decide whether the following statements are true (T) or false (F).

(1) China is the only country that celebrates the traditional Mid-Autumn Festival.

(2) For people in Guangdong Province, tidal bore watching is an important event on the Mid-Autumn day.

(3) The Chinese people's tradition of worshiping the moon and offering sacrifices to it can be traced back more than 1,000 years.

(4) People would hold activities to pray for blessings from the Moon Goddess on this day.

(5) In 2006, the holiday was added to the list of China's first batch of national intangible cultural heritages.

3. Translating

Translate the following paragraph into Chinese.

The Mid-Autumn Festival falls on the 15th day of the eighth lunar month. Since ancient times, people have celebrated it by worshipping and admiring the glorious full moon, and enjoying osmanthus flowers and fermented-osmanthus wine. The Chinese believe that the full moon represents family reunions. Therefore, Mid-Autumn Festival is also a day for families to get together and for those far away from home to think of their loved ones.

4. Developing Critical Thinking

Work in pairs and discuss the following questions.

(1) Why do people worship the moon during the Mid-Autumn Festival?

(2) How do you and your family celebrate the Mid-Autumn Festival?

Further Reading

The Qixi Festival Is More than Chinese Valentine's Day

While Valentine's Day is celebrated in many countries on February 14, the Qixi Festival is regarded as being China's Valentine's Day.

Falling on the seventh day of the seventh lunar month, the Qixi Festival, also widely known as Double Seventh Festival, takes place on August 17 this year.

The traditional festival which was added to China's National Intangible Cultural Heritage List in 2006, has a lineage of over 2,000 years.

However, not many people know that it originated as a festival for young ladies and the "real" Valentine's Day in ancient China was actually celebrated on the 15th day of the first lunar month — best known as the Lantern Festival.

The Qixi Festival was initially to highlight people's worship of nature and women's domestic skills. Only later did it become associated with romance thanks to a popular folktale of an ill-fated love between a cowherd and a weaving maid.

As with many traditional Chinese festivals, the romantic legend behind the day of love has endured for thousands of years.

The story goes that a warm-hearted cowherd called Niu Lang, who lost his parents and led a hard life with an old ox, fell in love with a girl named Zhi Nyu, a weaving maid who escaped from the heaven because its rigid rituals made her life dull. They got married, soon had two children and lived together happily for a few years.

However, Zhi Nyu's mother, the Empress of Heaven, was enraged to find that her daughter had married a mere mortal and sent soldiers to fetch her back.

The cowherd's friend, the old ox, decided to sacrifice itself and offer its skin so that the cowherd could use it and enter Heaven to find his wife.

When the devastated cowherd arrived in Heaven with the two kids, the Empress was furious and created a huge heavenly river in the sky to separate the lovers as a punishment.

The magpies in the land were deeply moved by the cowherd's pure love, so flew up to the Heavens and formed a bridge over the river.

Even the Empress was touched by the loyalty shown by the cowherd and eventually allowed him to meet her daughter on the magpie bridge every Double Seventh Day.

Eventually, the cowherd turned into the star Altair and his wife into the star Vega, forever shining in the sky as a mark of their love.

This romantic tale is told every year during the Qixi Festival to commemorate the eternal love between the cowherd and the weaving maid, to celebrate the reunion of their family and also to express their wishes for pure love.

Though the legendary love story makes the day a Chinese equivalent of Valentine's Day, the Qixi Festival, in essence, goes much farther and embraces more profound meanings.

The festival originated from ancient time when people worshiped and had great respect for nature and the cosmos. Writers from the Han Dynasty (206 BC – AD 220) personified the stars of Altair and Vega while describing the night view during the Qixi Festival in their works, which then evolved into the romantic myth.

The Qixi Festival was originally named "the Qiqiao Festival" — which means to pray for intelligence — and on the eve on Double Seventh Day, girls used to offer fruit, flowers and even their their sewing kits to the Altair and Vega stars, to pray for more wisdom and marital happiness.

Needlework is considered representative of mastering the domestic skills, which was very important for young girls in traditional Chinese culture, thus the young women would show their dexterity by speedily threading a needle under the moonlight on that day.

In addition to their sewing, they also prepared a table of offerings including tea, wine and fruits. Red dates, hazelnuts, peanuts and melon seeds were also offered to the stars to wish for a good husband, healthy children and a happy family.

As most of the traditional customs for the festival are related to young ladies, it obtained the nickname of "Daughters' Day," which was recorded for the first time during the Yuan Dynasty, and further highlighted the essential domestic role played by women.

Aside from the traditions involving sewing, people also made and ate a specialty called "skill fruit" — a kind of fried, thin pastry made into different shapes — to present their talent. Finally, the skill fruit biscuits would be threaded together by the red string and offered in batches. Today, the Qixi Festival is much more commercialized with meals, chocolates and flowers in a way that is similar to Valentine's Day, but it also includes other celebrations such as wearing traditional Han Chinese clothing and floating river lanterns to pay respect to traditional culture.

Chinese people, nowadays, still prepare offerings and enjoy the traditional fruit biscuits on this special day, not only just to celebrate love but to show their awe for the beauty of nature and to ask for wisdom and fortune.

(Source: https://news.cgtn.com/news/3d3d674e7859544e79457a6333566d54/index.html)

Keys to Exercises

Unit 1

Text A

1. (1) blueprint: a detailed outline or plan of action

(2) pandemic: an epidemic that is geographically widespread

(3) congress: a meeting of elected or appointed representatives

(4) harmony: a consistent, orderly, or pleasing arrangement of parts

(5) initiative: an important act or statement that is intended to solve a problem

(6) prosperity: a successful, flourishing, or thriving condition

(7) infrastructure: the basic structure or features of a system or organization

(8) telecommunication: systems used in transmitting messages over a distance electronically

2. (1) T   (2) F   (3) T   (4) T   (5) F

4. The world today is undergoing profound changes unseen in a century. Political multi-polarization, economic globalization, cultural diversity and the trend of IT application are irreversible. Countries are increasingly interconnected and interdependent, but they also face many common challenges. Non-traditional global security issues such as food security, resource shortage, climate change, cyber attacks, population explosion, environmental pollution, disease epidemics and transnational crimes have emerged one after another, posing grave challenges to the international order and the survival of mankind. No matter where people live, what they believe, or whether they want to, they are already in a community with a shared future. At the same time, a global value aimed at addressing the common challenges of mankind has begun to emerge and gradually gain international consensus.

Text B

1. (1) desertification (2) optimize (3) emission (4) formulate (5) thriving

(6) lush (7) mechanism (8) combat (9) momentum (10) manifest

2. (1) F   (2) T   (3) T   (4) F   (5) T

3. 作为世界第二大经济体和可再生能源领域的全球领导者，中国的绿色转型可惠及国内外数十亿人。难怪许多新兴经济体都在关注中国如何实现这一转型。而这一转型也是中国"十四五"规划（2021—2025年）的核心内容。人与自然如何共存共荣，取决于中国如何实现转型。

Unit 2

Text A

1. (1) endeavor: an attempt to do something

(2) aspiration: a strong desire to achieve things

(3) headquarters: the main offices of an organization, e.g., the police, or a business company

(4) blueprint: an early plan or design that explains how something might be achieved

(5) resilience: the ability to be happy, successful, etc. again after something difficult

(6) venture: a new activity, usually in business, that involves risk or uncertainty

(7) vitality: energy and strength

(8) coordinate: organize the different parts of an activity and the people involved in it

2. (1) T   (2) F   (3) T   (4) T   (5) F

4. Chinese modernization is the socialist modernization pursued under the leadership of the CPC. The Chinese modernization is rooted in China's realities and in keeping with the global trend. This modernization features peaceful development and harmony between man and nature, and will present new opportunities to the cooperation between China and other countries. It contains elements that are common to the modernization processes of all countries, but it is more characterized by features that are unique to the Chinese context.

Text B

1. (1) renown   (2) multipolar   (3) alleviation   (4) dialectic   (5) rejuvenation
(6) dedication   (7) pivot   (8) appalled   (9) plundered   (10) ushers

2. (1) F   (2) T   (3) T   (4) F   (5) T

3. 此外，中国的现代化在包括科技在内的其他领域也产生了广泛的影响。事实证明，中国在尖端空间技术方面是一支领先力量，发射了自己的卫星，执行了载人飞行任务，建造了自己的空间站。中国对人类进步的承诺远远超出了地球，因为中华民族追求对月球、火星和其他地方的和平探索。

Unit 3

Text A

1. (1) cohort: a group of people who share a characteristic, usually age

(2) implication: the effect that an action or decision will have on something else in the future

(3) allocate: to give something to someone as their share of a total amount

(4) impetus: something that encourages a particular activity

(5) transition: a change from one type to another, or the process by which this happens

(6) hub: the central or main part of something where there is most activity

(7) landmark: a building or place that you can use to judge where you are

(8) navigation: the skill or the process of planning a route for a ship or other vehicle and taking it there

2. (1) T   (2) F   (3) T   (4) F   (5) T

4. Traditional manufacturing is the foundation of the modern industrial system. We must accelerate the digitalization of traditional manufacturing, and apply advanced and appropriate technologies to make this sector higher-end, smarter, and more eco-friendly. We should promote research, development, and application of frontier technologies for new energy, artificial intelligence, biological manufacturing, green and low-carbon industries, and quantum computing and support the development of enterprises that use sophisticated technologies to produce novel and unique products.

Text B

1. (1) consecutive   (2) devastating   (3) legislation   (4) manufacturer   (5) deliberate
   (6) commission   (7) navigation   (8) deployed   (9) prominent   (10) forge

2. (1) F   (2) T   (3) T   (4) T   (5) F

3. 把党的二十大描绘的宏伟蓝图变成现实，需要各行各业青年勇挑重担、冲锋在前。希望你们继续弘扬航空报国精神，心往一处想，劲往一处使，在推动航空科技自立自强上奋勇攀登，在促进航空工业高质量发展上积极作为，争做有理想、敢担当、能吃苦、肯奋斗的新时代好青年，为全面建设社会主义现代化国家、全面推进中华民族伟大复兴作出新贡献。

Unit 4

Text A

1. (1) backdrop: the general situation in which particular events happen

   (2) catering: the business or activity of providing food and drink at events

   (3) trajectory: a path, progression, or line of development

   (4) resilience: the ability to recover after something bad has happened

   (5) capability: the ability or power to do something

   (6) manufacturing: the business of producing goods in large numbers

   (7) inflation: an increase in prices over time, causing a reduction in the value of money

   (8) consumption: the act of using, eating, or drinking something

2. (1) T   (2) F   (3) F   (4) T   (5) T

4. **Xiong'an China: A Millennial Plan of National Significance**

As China enters a new era, Xiong'an, thriving with strength and vigor, has drawn the attention of the whole world. The Xiong'an New Area sits at the heart of the triangular area formed by Beijing, Tianjin and Baoding, 105 kilometers away from both Beijing and Tianjin. It is part of the Beijing-Tianjin-Hebei region that boasts enormous economic potential. The strategy of coordinated development in this region, introduced in 2014, has been pushed forward with full steam and across the board. Xi Jinping, general secretary of the Communist Party of China Central Committe, pointed out that Xiong'an New Area will be a legacy for our future generations. Following the principle of global vision, international standards, Chinese characteristics, and high goals, we should aim to build a demonstration area that practices the new concept for development.

Text B

1. (1) optimized (2) proactive (3) tortuous (4) prudent (5) monetary
 (6) navigate (7) convened (8) leveraging (9) alleviate (10) defuse

2. (1) T (2) F (3) T (4) F (5) F

3. 中国政府部门正在加大对中小微企业及个体工商户的支持，通过一系列税费优惠政策的延期和优化，着力推动民营经济的发展。一系列税费优惠政策形成合力，有望助力中小微企业、个体工商户活力提升，改善企业经营状况，充分吸纳就业。

Unit 5

Text A

1. (1) tributary: a stream or river that flows into a larger river

(2) consecutive: numbers or periods of time follow one after another without an interruption

(3) eradicate: to completely get rid of something such as a disease or a social problem

(4) reservoir: a lake, where water is stored before it is supplied to people's houses

(5) jurisdiction: the right to use an official power to make legal decisions

(6) algae: a very simple plant without stems or leaves that grows in or near water

(7) laud: to praise someone or something

(8) mechanism: a system or a way of behaving that helps a living thing to avoid or protect itself from something difficult or dangerous

2. (1) F (2) T (3) F (4) T (5) F

4. We should protect the eco-environment as we protect our eyes, and cherish it as we cherish our own lives. We should lay the groundwork for long-term benefits, take concrete steps to protect nature, restore the ecosystems, and create a beautiful environment. We should make it possible for people to enjoy the natural landscape and retain their love of nature, while returning serenity, harmony and beauty back to nature.

Text B

1. (1) nurturing (2) mainstay (3) quest (4) garnered (5) trendy
 (6) streamline (7) authoritative (8) scoured (9) cutlery (10) succulent

2. (1) T (2) T (3) F (4) T (5) T

3. 我们坚持绿水青山就是金山银山的理念，坚持山水林田湖草沙一体化保护和系统治理，全方位、全地域、全过程加强生态环境保护，生态文明制度体系更加健全，污染防治攻坚向纵深推进，绿色、循环、低碳发展迈出坚实步伐，生态环境保护发生历史性、转折性、全局性变化，我们的祖国天更蓝、山更绿、水更清。

Unit 6

Text A

1. (1) cosmology: the study of the nature and origin of the universe

   (2) stilt: one of a set of long pieces of wood or metal used to support a building

   (3) cluster: a group of similar things that are close together

   (4) franchise: a right to sell a company's products using the company's name

   (5) configuration: the particular arrangement or pattern of a group of related things

   (6) heritage: features that were created in the past and still have historical importance

   (7) sincerity: honesty

   (8) ingenious: (of a person) clever, original and incentive

2. (1) T　　(2) F　　(3) F　　(4) T　　(5) F

4. Influenced by the Taoism, the ancients paid much attention to the realm of nature as well as harmony between human and nature. As the core of traditional local-style dwelling houses, courtyard space is a complex space of reality and fantasy. It attracts people to entertain guest, offer sacrifices to gods or ancestors, hold wedding ceremony, play game and enjoy the cool in this enclosed and open space. Therefore, in the layout of traditional courtyard space, the ancients often skillfully designed the dialogue between man and nature, and introduced rockery, water, flowers, grass, trees, etc. into the courtyard space enclosed on all sides and open on the top. Meanwhile, it imitated the natural scenery and designed the asymmetrical free space level by making use of light and darkness, space twists and turns, large and small scale, the seriousness and liveliness of the atmosphere as well as the separation and closure of the distance to create the free and romantic atmosphere of Taoism in the courtyard.

Text B

1. (1) unevenness　　(2) texture　　(3) revival　　(4) be fleshed out

   (5) dedicated　　(6) ingenuity　　(7) cooperate with　　(8) vitality

   (9) surveillance　　(10) be entrusted

2. (1) T　　(2) F　　(3) F　　(4) T　　(5) T

3. 　　红色是闽南建筑的生命，红墙、红瓦、红砖铺路。可以说闽南人离不开红色，红色是他们生活密不可分的一部分。取材以当地红土为主料，烧制成红砖、红瓦，成为闽南建筑独特的视觉特征。除了厦门、漳州、泉州的红色建筑区域特征最为明显外，莆田地区的古民居建筑和福清南部地区的古民居建筑也都属于此类红色建筑区域。

Unit 7

Text A

1. (1) garner: to collect something, usually after much work or with difficulty

(2) fabrics: cloth or material for making clothes, covering furniture, etc.

(3) intangible: that exists but that is difficult to describe, understand or measure

(4) craftsmanship: the level of skill shown by somebody in making something beautiful with their hands

(5) sate: to satisfy someone by giving them something that is wanted or needed

(6) dissolution: the act or process of ending an official organization or legal agreement

(7) rim: the outer, often curved or circular, edge of something

(8) innovation: the introduction of new things, ideas or ways of doing something

2. (1) T (2) T (3) F (4) T (5) T

4. China's new concept of civilization was created on the basis of traditional Chinese culture, particularly Hehe Culture. Its starting point and purpose are very different from those of the Clash of Civilizations theory. China champions equality, mutual learning, dialogue, and inclusiveness among civilizations. Respecting the diversity of world civilizations, China advocates that estrangement, clashes and superiority be replaced with exchanges, mutual learning and coexistence. Exchanges and mutual learning among civilizations should be deepened, so that all the people from different countries can understand each other in a friendly manner and face global challenges together. The civilization of each country and nation is deeply rooted in its soil, and has its own inherent characteristics, strengths and virtues. Great efforts should be exerted to preserve the diversity of civilizations, and enhance mutual communication, learning and reference, instead of mutual estrangement, exclusion and even displacement. Only in this way can the garden of world civilizations be full of vitality.

Text B

1. (1) prosperity   (2) privilege   (3) meticulous   (4) insurmountable   (5) pinnacle
(6) illiteracy   (7) recreational   (8) tend to   (9) auctioning   (10) aesthetic

2. (1) T (2) F (3) T (4) F (5) T

3. 文明交流互鉴，是中国处理不同文明的关系问题的基本立场。文明因多样而交流，因交流而互鉴，因互鉴而发展，这是中国新型文明观的集中体现。文明是社会发展进步的标志，也代表着不同社会形式的思想内涵和价值立场。因此，文明原本就应当是多元的而非单一的。

Unit 8

Text A

1. (1) regatta: a sports event consisting of boat races
   (2) delicacy: something especially rare or expensive that is good to eat
   (3) migrant: a person that travels to a different country, often in order to find work
   (4) timber: a long piece of wood used for building, especially houses and ships
   (5) knack: a skill or an ability to do something easily and well
   (6) collaboration: the situation of two or more people working together to create or achieve the same thing
   (7) paddle: to push a pole with a wide end through the water in order to make a boat move
   (8) sideline: a line that shows the position of the side of an area where a sport is played

2. (1) F (2) F (3) T (4) T (5) F

4. In ancient China, the Dragon Boat Festival was at the start of summer when diseases were more prevalent. Mugwort leaves were used as herbal medicine to combat such diseases. Their fragrance can drive away flies and mosquitoes. Calamus is an aquatic plant that has similar effects. On the fifth day of the fifth lunar month, people usually clean their houses, courtyards, and hang mugwort and calamus on lintels to ward off diseases. It is also said that hanging mugwort and calamus can bring good luck to the family.

Text B

1. (1) connotations (2) illuminated (3) overwhelmed (4) crisp (5) exquisite
   (6) thrive (7) feast (8) turbulence (9) worship (10) delicacies

2. (1) T (2) F (3) F (4) T (5) T

3. 农历八月十五是中秋节。自古以来，人们就通过拜月、赏月、赏桂花、饮桂花酒等方式来庆祝中秋佳节。中国人相信满月象征着家庭团聚，因此，中秋节是家人团聚的日子，也是那些远在异乡的人思念亲人的日子。